The Complete Book of Data Anonymization

From Planning to Implementation

Balaji Raghunathan

CRC Press
Taylor & Francis Group
Boca Raton   London   New York

CRC Press is an imprint of the
Taylor & Francis Group, an **informa** business
AN AUERBACH BOOK

CRC Press
Taylor & Francis Group
6000 Broken Sound Parkway NW, Suite 300
Boca Raton, FL 33487-2742

International Standard Book Number: 978-1-4398-7730-2 (Hardback)

This book contains information obtained from authentic and highly regarded sources. Reasonable efforts have been made to publish reliable data and information, but the author and publisher cannot assume responsibility for the validity of all materials or the consequences of their use. The authors and publishers have attempted to trace the copyright holders of all material reproduced in this publication and apologize to copyright holders if permission to publish in this form has not been obtained. If any copyright material has not been acknowledged please write and let us know so we may rectify in any future reprint.

Library of Congress Cataloging-in-Publication Data

Raghunathan, Balaji.
 The complete book of data anonymization : from planning to implementation / Balaji Raghunathan.
  pages cm
  Includes bibliographical references and index.
  ISBN 978-1-4398-7730-2 (hardcover : alk. paper)
  1. Data protection. 2. Database security. 3. Database management. 4. Computer security. I. Title.

 QA76.9.A25.R338 2013
 005.8--dc23   2012030990

Visit the Taylor & Francis Web site at
http://www.taylorandfrancis.com

and the CRC Press Web site at
http://www.crcpress.com

Contents

Introduction

As a data anonymization and data privacy protection solution architect, I have spent a good amount of time understanding how data anonymization, as a data privacy protection measure, is being approached by enterprises across different industrial sectors. Most of these enterprises approached enterprise-wide data anonymization more as an art than as a science.

Despite the initiation of data privacy protection measures like enterprise-wide data anonymization, a large number of enterprises still ran the risk of misuse of sensitive data by mischievous insiders. Though these enterprises procured advanced tools for data anonymization, many applications across the enterprise still used copies of actual production data for software development life cycle activities. The reasons for the less-than-expected success of data anonymization initiatives arose due to challenges arising from multiple quarters, ranging from technology to data to process to people.

This book intends to demystify data anonymization, identify the typical challenges faced by enterprises when they embark on enterprisewide data anonymization initiatives, and outline the best practices to address these challenges. This book recognizes that the challenges faced by the data anonymization program sponsor/manager are different from those of a data anonymization practitioner. The program sponsor's worries are more about getting the program executed on time and on budget and ensuring the continuing success of the program as a whole whereas the practitioner's challenges are more technological or application-specific in nature.

Part I of this book is for the anonymization program sponsor, who can be the CIO or the IT director of the organization. In this part, this book describes the need for data anonymization, what data anonymization is, when to go in for data anonymization, how a data anonymization program should be scoped, what the challenges are when planning for this initiative at an enterprise-level scope, who in the organization needs to be involved in the program, which are the processes that need to be set up, and what operational aspects to watch out for.

Part II of this book is for the data anonymization practitioner, who can be a data architect, a technical lead, or an application architect. In this part, this book describes the different solution patterns and techniques available for data anonymization, how to select a pattern and a technique, the step-by-step approach toward data anonymization for an application, the challenges encountered, and the best practices involved.

This book is not intended to help design and develop data anonymization algorithms or techniques or build data anonymization tools. This book should be thought of more as a reference guide for data anonymization implementation.

Acknowledgments

More than an individual effort, this book is the result of the contributions of many people.

I would like to thank the key contributors:

Jophy Joy, from Infosys, for granting me permission to use all of the cartoons in this book. Jophy, who describes himself as a passionate "virus" for cartooning, has brought to life through his cartoons the lighter aspects of data anonymization, and has made the book more colorful.

Sandeep Karamongikar, from Infosys, for being instrumental in introducing me to the world of data anonymization, providing early feedback on the book, and ensuring executive support and guidance in publishing the book.

Venugopal Subbarao, from Infosys, for agreeing to review the book despite his hectic schedule, and providing expert guidance and comments, which helped shape this book.

Swaminathan Natarajan and Ramakrishna G. Reddy, from Infosys, for review of the book from a technical perspective.

Dr. Ramkumar Ramaswamy, from Performance Engineering Associates, as well as Ravindranath P. Hirolikar, Vishal Saxena, Shanmugavel S. and Santhosh G. Ramakrishna, from Infosys, for reviewing select chapters and providing their valuable comments.

Prasad Joshi, from Infosys, for providing executive support and guidance and ensuring that my official work assignments did not infringe on the time reserved for completing the book.

Dr. Pramod Varma, from Unique Identification Authority of India, for reading through the book and providing his valuable inputs on data privacy, and helping me with ideas for another book!!

Subu Goparaju and Dr. Anindya Sircar, from Infosys, for their executive guidance and support in publishing the book.

Sudhanshu Hate, from Infosys, and Parameshwaran Seshan, an independent trainer and consultant, for guiding me through the procedural aspects of getting the book published.

Dr. Praveen Bhasa Malla, from Infosys, for assisting me in getting this book published, right from the conceptual stage of the book.

Subramanya S.V., Dr. Sarma K.V.R.S., and Chidananda B. Gurumallappa, from Infosys, for their guidance in referencing external content in the book.

This book would not have been possible without the help received from Rich O'Hanley, Laurie Schlags, Michele A. Dimont, Deepa Jagdish, Kary A. Budyk, Elise Weinger, and Bill Pacheco, from Taylor & Francis. They patiently answered several of my queries and guided me through the entire journey of getting this book published.

I would also like to express my gratitude to Dr. Ten H. Lai, of Ohio State University, Cassie Stevenson, from Symantec, Susan Jayson, from Ponemon Institute, as well as Helen Wilson, from *The Guardian*, for providing me permission to reference content in my book.

I would like to dedicate this effort of writing a book to my father, P.K. Raghunathan, mother, Kalyani, wife, Vedavalli T.V., 8-year-old daughter, Samhitha, and 3-year-old son, Sankarshan, who waited for me for several weekends over a period of more than a year to finish writing this book and spend time with them. Their understanding and patience helped me concentrate on the book and get it out in due time.

Concerted efforts have been made to avoid any copyright violations. Wherever needed, permission has been sought from copyright owners. Adequate care has been taken in citing the right sources and references. However, should there be any errors or omissions, they are inadvertent and I apologize for the same. I would be grateful for such errors to be brought to my attention so that they can be incorporated in the future reprints or editions of this work.

I acknowledge the proprietary rights of the trademarks and the product names of the companies mentioned in the book.

About the Author

Balaji Raghunathan has more than 15 years of experience in the software industry and has spent a large part of his working career in software architecture and information management. He has been with Infosys for the last 10 years.

In 2009, Raghunathan was introduced to data anonymization and ever since has been fascinated by this art and science of leaving users in doubt as to whether the data are real or anonymized. He is convinced that this is a valuable trick enterprises need to adopt in order to prevent misuse of personal data they handle and he has helped some of Infosys clients play these tricks systematically.

He is a TOGAF 8.0 and ICMG-WWISA Certified Software Architect and has worked on data anonymization solutions for close to two years in multiple roles. Prior to 2009, Raghunathan has been involved in architecting software solutions for the energy, utilities, publishing, transportation, retail, and banking industries.

Raghunathan has a postgraduate diploma in business administration (finance) from Symbiosis Institute (SCDL), Pune, India and has an engineering degree (electrical and electronics) from Bangalore University, India.

1

OVERVIEW OF DATA ANONYMIZATION

Points to Ponder

- What is data anonymization?
- What are the drivers for data anonymization?

Here are some startling statistics on security incidents and private data breaches:

- Leading technology and business research firms report that 70% of all security incidents and 80% of threats come from insiders and 65% are undetected.[1]
- *The Guardian* reports that a leading healthcare provider in Europe has suffered 899 personal data breach incidences between 2008–2011[2] and also reports that the biggest threat to its data security is its staff.[3]
- Datalossdb, a community research project aimed at documenting known and reported data loss incidents worldwide, reports that in 2011:
  - A major entertainment conglomerate found 77 million customer records had been compromised.[4]
  - A major Asian developer and media network had the personal information of 6.4 million users compromised.[4]
  - An international Asian bank had the personal information of 20,000 customers compromised.[4]

The growing incidence of misuse of personal data has resulted in a slew of data privacy protection regulations by various governments across countries. The primary examples of these regulations include the European Data Protection Directive and its local derivatives, the U.S. Patriot Act, and HIPAA.

Mischievous insiders selling confidential data of customer. (Courtesy of Jophy Joy)

The increasing trend of outsourcing software application development and testing to remote offshore locations has also increased the risk of misuse of sensitive data and has resulted in another set of regulations such as PIPEDA (introduced by the Canadian government).

These regulations mandate protection of sensitive data involving personally identifiable information (PII) and protected health information (PHI) from unauthorized personnel. Unauthorized personnel include the application developers, testers, and any other users not mandated by business to have access to these sensitive data.

The need to comply with these regulations along with the risk of hefty fines and potential loss of business in the event of misuse of personal data of customers, partners, and employees by insiders have led to enterprises looking at data privacy protection solutions such as anonymization. Data anonymization ensures that even if (anonymized) data are stolen, they cannot be used (misused)!!

PII

PII is any information which, by itself, or when combined with additional information, enables identification or inference of the individual. As a rule of thumb, any personally identifiable information that in the hands of a wrong person has the potential for loss of reputation or blackmail, should be protected as PII.

PII EXAMPLES

PII includes the following attributes.

Financial: Credit card number, CVV1, CVV2, account number, account balance, or credit balance

Employment related: Salary details

Personal: Photographs, iris scan, biometric details, national identification number such as SSN, national insurance number, tax identification number, date of birth, age, gender, marital status, religion, race, address, zip code, city, state, vehicle registration number, and driving license details

Educational details: such as qualifications, university course, school or college studied, year of passing

Contact information: including e-mail address, social networking login, telephone number (work, residential, mobile)

Medical information: Prior medical history/pre-existing diseases, patient identification number

PII DEFINITION

The National Institute of Standards and Technology (NIST) defines PII as any information that allows

- **Tracing of an individual or distinguishing of an individual:** This is the information which by itself identifies an individual. For example, national insurance number, SSN, date of birth, and so on.[5]

or

- **Linked or linkable information about the individual:** This is the information associated with the individual. For example, let's assume a scenario where the first name and educational details are stored in one data store, and the last name and educational details are in another data

> store. If the same individual can always access both data stores, this individual can link the information to identify another individual. This is a case of linked information. If the same individual cannot access both data stores at the same time, or needs to access both data stores separately, it is a case of linkable information.[5]

Thus if both data stores do not have controls that allow for segregation of data stores, it is an example of linked information. If the data stores have segregating security controls, it is linkable information.

PHI

A lot of personal health information is collected, generated, stored, or transmitted by healthcare providers. This may be past health information, present health information, or future health information of an individual. Health may point toward physical or mental health or both. Such information directly or indirectly identifies the individual. The difference between PII and PHI is that PHI does not include education or employment attributes. The introduction of the Health Insurance Portability and Accountability Act (HIPAA) by the United States brought in the necessary urgency among organizations toward protection of PHI. PHI covers all forms of media (electronic, paper, etc.).

What Is Data Anonymization?

Data anonymization is the process of de-identifying sensitive data while preserving its format and data type.

The masked data can be realistic or a random sequence of data. Or the output of anonymization can be deterministic, that is, the same value every time. All these are dependent on the technique used for anonymization.

Technically, data masking refers to a technique that replaces the data with a special character whereas data anonymization or data obfuscation constitutes hiding of data and this would imply replacement of the original data value with a value preserving the format and type. Thus, replacing "Don Quixote" with "Ron Edwards" would be a case of data anonymization whereas replacing "Don Quixote" with "XXXXXXXXXXX" would be a case of data masking.

However, colloquially, data masking, data anonymization, data de-identification, and data obfuscation are interchangeably used and hence in this book, for all purposes, data anonymization and data masking are used interchangeably. In this book, when we are looking at data masking technically, "character masking technique" would be explicitly mentioned.

What Are the Drivers for Data Anonymization?

The need for data anonymization can be attributed to the following key drivers:

- The need to protect sensitive data generated as part of business
- Increasing instances of misuse of personal data and resultant privacy issues
- Astronomical cost to the business due to misuse of personal data
- Risks arising out of operational factors such as outsourcing and partner collaboration
- Legal and compliance requirements

The Need to Protect Sensitive Data Handled as Part of Business

Today's enterprises handle enormous amounts of sensitive data as part of their business. The sensitive data can be the personally identifiable information of customers collected as part of their interactions with them, the personally identifiable information of employees including salary details collected as part of their HR (Human Resource) processes, or protected health information of their customers and employees. Enterprises collect, store, and process these data and may need to exchange these data with their partners, outsourcing vendors. Misuse of any of this information poses a serious threat to their business. In addition to PII and PHI, enterprises also handle a lot of classified information that should not be made available to the public or to partners or to competitors and these also need to be protected from any misuse.

*Increasing Instances of Insider Data Leakage, Misuse of Personal
Data, and the Lure of Money for Mischievous Insiders*

Based on its research from various cybercrime forums, a leading U.S.
newspaper has found interesting statistics on the black market of
private data. The study shows that leaking the driver's license information of one person can fetch between $100–$200, and billing data,
SSN, date of birth, and credit card number can fetch a higher price.[6]

With such a booming black market for personally identifiable
information, it is no wonder that the incidences of misuse of personal
data by insiders have increased.

Misuse of personal data can be intentional or unintentional.

Employees Getting Even with Employers   Monetary gain is not the sole
motivator for misuse of personal data by insiders. Cases have come
to light where dissatisfied employees or contractors have leaked or
misused personal data of customers just to get back at the company or
organization. This has resulted in a serious loss of image and business
to these companies.

Employees getting even with employers. (Courtesy of Jophy Joy)

Negligence of Employees to Sensitivity of Personal Data   Concerns related
to loss of privacy of customers, partners, and employees have not
arisen just due to intentional misuse of customers' personal data.

Employee or organizational negligence has also contributed to this. The need to appear helpful to those asking for personal information, lack of sensitivity when dealing with personal data, absence of information privacy policies, or lack of adherence to information privacy policies of companies due to minimal awareness have all contributed to the misuse of personal data. Despite privacy regulations being passed by various governments, we still see organizations using the personal data of customers collected for business purposes for marketing activities and many customers are still unaware of this.

Negligence of employees regarding sensitivity of personal data. (Courtesy of Jophy Joy)

Astronomical Cost to the Business Due to Misuse of Personal Data

In addition to loss of customer trust and resultant attrition, any misuse of personal data of customers or employees involves the need to engage lawyers for legal defense. Most cases of personal data misuse also end up in hefty fines for the enterprises thus making the cost extremely expensive.

In March 2011, Ponemon Institute, a privacy think tank, published their sixth annual study findings on the cost of data breaches to U.S.-based companies. This benchmark study was sponsored by Symantec and involved detailed research on the data breach experiences of more than 50 U.S. companies cutting across different industry sectors

Table 1.1 Estimated Cost of Data Breach[7]

DESCRIPTION	ESTIMATE
Cost of every compromised customer record per data breach incident	$214
Average total cost per incident	$7.2 Million
Average customer churn rates (loss of customers who were affected by the data breach incident after being notified of this breach)	4%

including healthcare, finance, retail, services, education, technology, manufacturing, transportation, hotels and leisure, entertainment, pharmaceuticals, communications, energy, and defense.

Each of the data breach incidents involved about 1,000 to 100,000 records being compromised. This study arrived at an estimate of the per-customer record cost and average per-incident cost, as well as the customer churn rate as a result of the breach. The figures are shown in Table 1.1.

The direct cost factors that have gone into the above estimate include expensive mechanisms for detection, escalation, notification, and response in addition to legal, investigative, and administrative expenses, customer support information hotlines, and credit monitoring subscriptions. The indirect or resultant cost factors include customer defections, opportunity loss, and reputation management.

Risks Arising out of Operational Factors Such as Outsourcing and Partner Collaboration

Outsourcing of IT application development, testing, and support activities result in data moving out of the organization's own premises as well as data being accessible to employees of the contracted organizations.

Collaboration with partners increasingly involves exchange of data. For example, a healthcare company would need to exchange patient data with the health insurance provider.

Thus outsourcing and partner collaboration increases the risk of misuse of personal data manifold.

Legal and Compliance Requirements

When governments and regulatory bodies get their act together, they bring in legislation that ensures the risk of litigation remains high for businesses. Businesses respond by turning back to their legal department to ensure that they comply with the new regulations. Most governments have a "herd mentality" especially when it comes to issues that are global or have the potential to become global. When one friendly country passes legislation, it is just a matter of time before another country's government passes similar legislation.

This is what happened to "Protection of Data Privacy." The frequent incidents around identity theft and misuse of sensitive data ensured that the European Union passed the European Data Protection Directive and each of the countries belonging to the Union passed its own version of the European Data Protection Act. Meanwhile, the United States passed the "Patriot Act," the HIPAA, and Gramm–Leach–Bliley Act (GLBA), and Canada passed the PIPEDA act. All these acts focused on protection of sensitive personal data or protected health data.

Not to be left behind, the payment card industry came up with its own data security standards for protecting the consumer's credit card information. This set of standards was called "PCI-DSS" and imposed hefty fines on retailers and financial institutions in case of a data breach related to consumer credit cards. However, they also incentivize the retailers and financial institutions for adopting PCI-DSS (and showing evidence of this). Implementation of PCI-DSS on their IT systems lessens the probability of leakage or misuse of consumer credit card information. An overview of the privacy laws is provided in later chapters.

Although most security experts would put regulatory compliance as the primary driver for data anonymization, this has been listed as the last driver in this book as the increasing risk of misuse of personal data by insiders and increasing operational risks adopted by businesses led governments and regulatory bodies to pass data privacy legislation.

Will Procuring and Implementing a Data Anonymization Tool by Itself Ensure Protection of Privacy of Sensitive Data?

From a data privacy protection perspective, data anonymization is only one of the popular approaches used. Other approaches like data loss prevention, data tokenization, etc., may also be used for specific data privacy protection requirements.

Data anonymization addresses data privacy protection by hiding the personal dimension of data or information. However, the implementation of only data anonymization (using data anonymization tools) without the support of policies, processes, and people will be inadequate.

There are companies who have used SQL scripts efficiently to encrypt data and have seen a fairly successful data anonymization implementation, although on a smaller scale. There are also companies whose initiatives have failed after procurement of the best data masking tool on the market. For protection from misuse of personal data, processes and policies need to come together along with the anonymization tool and the human aspect.

Employee training and increasing the awareness of information security and privacy guidelines and policies have played a positive role in enterprises being able to bring down insider data breaches due to negligence.

Some of the reasons for limited success or failure of data anonymization implementation include the following:

Ambiguity of Operational Aspects

Important decisions such as who is supposed to mask data, who can see unmasked data, and who can use the masking tool are not clearly defined.

Allowing the Same Users to Access Both Masked and Unmasked Environments

There are organizations that allow developers/testers/contractors access to unmasked data and have the same personnel mask these data and further use the masked or anonymized data only for development/ testing on their premises. This defeats the purpose of anonymization.

Lack of Buy-In from IT Application Developers, Testers, and End-Users

Many implementations do not use a practical approach to data anonymization and do not secure the necessary buy-in from IT application developers, testers, and end-users before implementation and as a result end up with testers who refuse to test with masked data as they are not realistic. A practical approach implies alignment with the organization's localized processes and procedures associated with its businesses, IT applications, and dataflow.

Compartmentalized Approach to Data Anonymization

Many large enterprises have different departments using different anonymization tools and approaches and the organization ends up not being able to perform an integration test with masked data.

Absence of Data Privacy Protection Policies or Weak Enforcement of Data Privacy Policies

Although most companies do know that customer names, date of birth, and national identification numbers need to be masked, there is no policy surrounding what type of data fields must be anonymized. Many companies lack the will to enforce the policy on employees not following the privacy policy guidelines, until a breach occurs. Without any supporting governance structure, data security and privacy policy, access control policies, and buy-in from a large section of IT employees that includes application developers and testers, data anonymization initiatives are bound to fail.

The next set of chapters provides a view on how data anonymization programs can be successfully implemented with supporting tools, processes, and people along with a set of patterns and antipatterns.

Benefits of Data Anonymization Implementation

Any security- or risk-related initiative will not result in an increase in generated revenues. It is only an insurance against "known" attacks that can bring down a business. Thus data anonymization implementation can help only in the protection of data privacy. It can ensure that nonproduction users cannot make use of the data while allowing them to continue using the application with same functionality as it exists in a production environment.

A piecemeal approach to data anonymization has its own pitfalls, however, data anonymization implemented in the right way with all the supporting features across the enterprise has the following benefits:

- It reduces the likelihood of misuse of personal data by insiders and thereby the chance of litigation, especially when data are used in nonproduction environments.
- It increases adherence to data privacy laws and reduces hefty fines that may arise out of any misuse of personal data.
- More and more insurance companies are insuring their corporate customers only when they have a data security and privacy policy in place. Data anonymization, implemented the right way, should help reduce insurance premiums (by providing evidence of data security and privacy policy adherence) when insuring against data risks to the business.

A data anonymization program implemented at an enterprise level helps in standardization of data anonymization and privacy protection processes across the enterprise as well as reduction of operational cost of data anonymization.

Conclusion

Increasing incidences of insider data thefts and misuse of personal information of customers and employees have resulted in introduction of data privacy legislation by various governments and regulatory bodies. These pieces of legislation have made the cost of noncompliance and breach of personal data very expensive for businesses.

Although external attacks and hacker attacks on an enterprise can be prevented by network and physical security mechanisms, prevention of misuse of sensitive data can be achieved only by concerted data anonymization programs encompassing governance, processes, training, tools, techniques, and data security and privacy policy formulations.

References

1. Camouflage (http://doc.wowgao.com/ef/presentations/PPCamouflage.ppt)
2. *Guardian* (http://www.guardian.co.uk/healthcare-network/2011/may/04/personal-data-breaches-london-nhs-trusts data)

3. *Guardian* (http://www.guardian.co.uk/healthcare-network/2011/may/04/
   biggest-threat-nhs-data-security-staff)
4. Datalossdb (http://www.datalossdb.org)
5. NIST (*Guide to Protecting the Confidentiality of Personally Identifiable
   Information*)
6. *USA Today* (cybercrime forum) (http://www.usatoday.com/tech/news/
   computersecurity/infotheft/2006-10-11-cybercrime-hacker-forums_
   x.htm)
7. *2010 Annual Study: U.S. Cost of a Data Breach* (Research conducted by
   Ponemon Institute. LLC and Sponsored by Symantec)

PART I
DATA ANONYMIZATION PROGRAM SPONSOR'S GUIDEBOOK

This part of the book is meant for the sponsor of an enterprisewide data anonymization program who may be a CIO or an IT director. This part discusses the focus areas for the sponsor and the activities he or she should plan for at different stages of the data anonymization initiative.

In Chapter 2, we start off with the governance model, typically followed by organizations that have embarked on enterprisewide data anonymization programs.

We then move on to the most important prerequisite for a successful enterprisewide data anonymization implementation, namely, classification of enterprise data. In Chapter 3, we understand why we need to classify data and how we classify data.

After discussions on classification of enterprise data, we continue with Chapter 4 to see how the ecosystem of enterprisewide data privacy policies, guidelines, and processes need to complement data anonymization in order to protect against misuse of data, which the enterprise considers as sensitive.

We then move on to Chapter 5, where we discuss the "core" of the enterprisewide data anonymization implementation and understand the different phases an enterprisewide data anonymization implementation needs to go through.

After having a look at the end-to-end lifecycle of an enterprisewide data anonymization program, we look at how different departments in the enterprise need to be involved for the continued success of the program in Chapter 6.

In Chapter 7, we take a look at the data privacy maturity model or the data privacy meter, which helps us understand the different data privacy maturity levels and help spot where the enterprise stands in the model and where the enterprisewide data anonymization program should start from.

We then move on to Chapter 8 where we discuss different execution models for implementing data anonymization across the enterprise and identify the appropriate execution model for the enterprise.

After understanding the execution model for enterprisewide data anonymization, we take a look in Chapter 9 at whether we need a data anonymization tool for the enterprise, and understand how to short list the suitable data anonymization tools for the enterprise and arrive at a criteria for evaluating the best-fit data anonymization tool among the shortlisted ones.

While Chapter 5 discussed the end-to-end enterprise data anonymization lifecycle, we need to understand the granular activities involved in the implementation of data anonymization for an individual application. Chapter 10 provides an overview of the application-level anonymization activities and the high-level approach for estimating this effort for these activities.

Chapter 11, the final chapter in Part I, highlights the areas from where the next set of data privacy challenges for an enterprise would arise from.

2
ENTERPRISE DATA PRIVACY GOVERNANCE MODEL

Points to Ponder

- What is the appropriate governance model for data privacy protection?
- Which are the roles to be accommodated in the governance model?
- How does the governance model for data privacy protection influence the anonymization initiative?
- What are the dependencies on the employee for success of any data privacy protection initiative?

Although confidential information can be leaked by social engineering or even by somebody losing a piece of paper, misuse of personal data from information systems causes more widespread media coverage and results in the most conspicuous loss of reputation. Enforcing appropriate privacy practices across the enterprise needs a strong governance model with defined roles and responsibilities.

In this chapter, the word "privacy," when independently used, implies "data privacy." In order to keep the scope of the book limited to data anonymization and its ecosystem, the responsibilities of each role in the governance model are examined from a data anonymization perspective only (though there are other data privacy protection techniques like data tokenization and data loss prevention).

The governance model must assign accountability to different roles and must aid the accomplishment of the following objectives:

- Introduce measures for protection of data privacy across the enterprise.
- Ensure that data anonymization programs do not hinder the as-is development or as-is business processes.
- Manage change.

The job of a risk officer. (Courtesy of Jophy Joy)

- Ensure continuing management support to data privacy protection process implementation.
- Data privacy protection policy enforcement and controls.
- Handle incident response.
- Formulate policies on how to deal with employees and contractors not adhering to policies and frame policies for handling exceptions in consultation with legal team.
- Assign privacy responsibilities to data owners.
- Ensure alignment of anonymization policies and procedures with departments instead of one-size-fits-all policies and procedures.
- Review data access and data dissemination policy and controls.
- Evaluate risk, cost, and benefits of the anonymization program and take appropriate mitigation steps at each inflection point.

A typical data privacy governance model followed by large enterprises include the individual department/unit privacy compliance officers as well as the steering committee for data privacy protection initiatives (like data anonymization) and data privacy incident response team reporting to the chief privacy officer of the enterprise. The steering committee consists of representatives from management, information security/risk departments along with individual department/unit compliance officers.

A typical governance model for data privacy preservation looks like that in Figure 2.1.

Chief Privacy Officer

The reliability and trustworthiness of an organization is reflected by how securely the personal data collected, stored, and processed

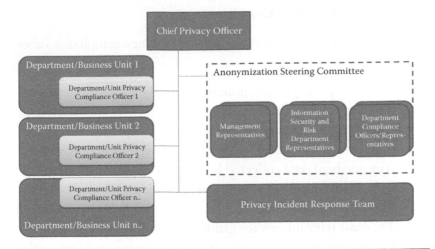

Figure 2.1   A typical governance model for privacy protection in an enterprise.

by the organization are managed. The chief privacy officer (CPO) is accountable not only for providing oversight of privacy practices across the enterprise, but also ensuring that the organization's privacy standards meet the high expectations of their customers and stakeholders with respect to protection of their personal information.

The CPO needs to work with the department/unit privacy compliance officer (or unit security and compliance officer) to review the state of the organization's privacy protection initiatives and help ensure that enterprise privacy policies meet the privacy objectives of the organization in an effective manner. The CPO also needs to ensure that the right privacy culture pervades the organization.

A culture of concern for privacy of customers and employees is promoted using a mix of incentivizing the employees as well as strong-arm tactics. In order to make employees understand the importance of managing risk, which includes treating the personal data of customers, partners, and employees with enough care, many organizations have also introduced risk management as part of the employees' performance appraisal process. There are organizations who believe that tying this to performance goals ensures that employees are aware of what they should do in order to mitigate the risk of handling sensitive data in their daily activities.

In many enterprises, the functions of chief privacy officer, chief data officer, chief risk officer, and chief security officer are all combined into one role.

Unit/Department Privacy Compliance Officers

The key mandate of the unit/department privacy compliance officers is to ensure that:

- The enterprise privacy policies are tailored to the needs of different roles in the department.
- Employees are trained on privacy policies and are aware of the importance of handling personal data with appropriate care.
- Any personal data collected by the unit/department as part of its business purposes is handled securely and is used only for the intended purpose.
- The most relevant privacy guidelines, policies, and procedures for employees that are within their business unit are easily accessible as per the role of the employees.
- The business unit will have specific privacy-related procedures and policies that guide the employees in their daily transactions. The policies and procedures should be easily accessible to the employees and should specify what is expected from the employee with respect to privacy compliance for each role.
- Training sessions on privacy policy adherence for employees and managers of the department are conducted regularly. The objective of the training should be to:
  - Equip individual managers to answer any compliance-related query of an employee.
  - Foster a privacy-sensitive culture among the employees.
  - Work with the HR (human resources) team to ensure that employees mandatorily attend the privacy compliance training once or twice every year.

The Steering Committee for Data Privacy Protection Initiatives

The steering committee for governing data privacy protection initiatives (such as data anonymization program implementation) includes representatives from management, information security, risk department, and department security and privacy compliance officers.

As the focus of this book is primarily on the implementation of an anonymization program for data privacy protection, only the description of how the steering committee works in the context of an anonymization program has been provided.

Management Representatives

The management representatives on the governance board perform the following:

- Ensure that change arising out of anonymization implementation is managed properly.
- Ensure continuing support of senior management toward implementation of anonymization across the enterprise.
- Ensure accountability of data owners and assign responsibilities (relevant to their application) to them.
- Constantly evaluate risks to the anonymization program and take mitigation steps.
- Get the costs of anonymization implementation approved by financial controllers.
- Articulate benefits of the data anonymization implementation program to influential naysayers in the organization.
- Define the eligibility criteria for a person to be nominated as a member of this governance board.

Information Security and Risk Department Representatives

The information security and risk department representatives perform the following:

- Review data privacy audit and compliance reports across the enterprise.
- Review implementation and maintenance of enterprisewide data privacy policies (in addition to data security policies).
- Review enforcement of data privacy policy and controls across the organization.
- Work with legal team for handling cases where a department, employee, partner, or a customer does not follow or refuses to follow privacy guidelines as well as handling of exception cases.
- Review sensitive data/information dissemination policy and controls.

*Representatives from the Departmental Security
and Privacy Compliance Officers*

The compliance officers work with the information security and risk representatives to have the data privacy policies and procedures tailored to the needs of their individual departments and enable access to the department's privacy policy database to employees as per their role.

In addition to the above, the steering committee may also have representatives from the CFO, organization, and legal department apart from the lead program manager of the anonymization program as members during the program implementation. The application owners and business analysts can be guest invitees whenever the anonymization of that application comes in for review. Some of the steering committees also include representatives from the tool vendor and the service implementation vendor.

Incident Response Team

Any privacy protection governance initiative can only minimize misuse of personal data to a large extent and 100% privacy protection cannot be achieved. It is always better to have an incident response team prepared for handling such occurrences. This team will also be tasked with interacting with media lest they sensationalize the incident.

The key objective of the incident response team is to ensure that the enterprise has the systems and processes to enable fast response to any privacy breach. The typical incident response team consists of:

- A set of incident handlers with the technical capability to identify the source and extent of the breach. They must be able to leverage security testing and forensic tools to identify the cause and the impact of the incident, ensure monitoring of systems across the enterprise for any breach, use a ticketing system to raise a ticket or investigate the breach reported in the ticketing systems, and notify the appropriate persons. Incident handlers sometimes need the help of application subject matter experts for understanding the breached application details.
- A legal representative with expertise in handling high-technology crimes to advise on the actions needed to be taken by the organization as per relevant privacy laws.

- A corporate communications representative to report the incident to the external world using the right channel and to handle the media.

Given that such incidences may have originated from rogue insiders, the human resources department may also have to be involved as part of this team to take action against the offenders.

There is a high overlap between security and privacy. In most organizations, the incidence response team for both security and privacy-related incidents is the same. Outsourced security service providers are increasingly being engaged by organizations to provide the technical capabilities for identifying the source of the incident and the internal team only consists of representatives from legal, corporate communications, information security, and risk departments (and occasionally representatives from human resources and application subject matter experts) for interactions with the external world.

The Role of the Employee in Privacy Protection

No governance model brings in the necessary changes unless the employees are trained to handle sensitive data carefully as part of their daily transactions.

The employees must ensure that personal data of customers and employees are provided the highest level of security and protection during daily usage as well as disposal. They must recognize that the data they handle are a vital asset for their organization and ensure that they are handled with the right level of security and care. Unless there are legal requirements or unless an authorized person requests the data, data should not be disclosed by any employee. As part of their daily work, employees must ensure the following:

- The highest level of security for personal data.
- The appropriate level of protection is provided to personal data during transmission, storage, and disposal.
- Only those data needed for the business must be collected and it is always better to not collect extra personal information.

The organization must also have the appropriate platform ready to enable employees to report suspicious practices and incidents especially with respect to handling personal data. In case of any doubts, they should contact their manager or their unit compliance officer. For their part, organizations must make it easy for employees to consult the relevant person for clarification on any day-to-day transactions requiring handling of personal data as per their governance model. Access to any repository containing the privacy policies and practices relevant to each role must be made available to them.

The Role of the CIO

Given the all-pervasive nature of data and information across an enterprise, no committee is complete without a CIO. A CIO would remain the key stakeholder for any data privacy initiative.

Typical Ways Enterprises Enforce Privacy Policies

Many organizations disable employee access to the organization's information systems until the employee attends the mandatory privacy compliance training. This training spans all roles across the enterprise. The objective of this training program is to create awareness among the employees (as well as contractors and partners) on what is meant by PII, what is the sensitive data they handle as part of their daily interactions with the external world, why they should handle sensitive data with care, and their responsibility toward protecting these data.

The enterprises also have a test or a quiz conducted at the end of the training and require the employees to get more than half of the answers right. If not, they require the employee to attend the training again until he or she is able to get answers for at least half the questions right.

In order to enforce a strong data privacy protection culture, many enterprises require adherence to strong data privacy policies as part of their employee code of conduct.

Conclusion

The organization needs personal data of its employees and customers for their business processes. In order to prevent any misuse of personal data, organizations need to adhere to a set of guidelines:

The organization must ensure that it collects from their customers and employees only those attributes of personal information which are an absolute must for their business processes. Once collected, the organization must ensure that the information is stored, transmitted, and disposed of with the highest possible safety and security standards.

The personal data must be collected only after the customer/employee agrees to the usage purposes stated by the organization in the contract with the customer or employee and should not be used for other purposes. These data should be used only for those purposes as have been explicitly communicated to the customers or employees.

Any personal data being transmitted to third-party providers or partners must also be mentioned in the contract. Some of the privacy regulations treat the organization to be considered responsible in the case of data leakage or misuse even if the source of the misuse is the partner or vendor organizations.

The organization must also ensure the right to the personal data collected to the owner of the data (customer or employee) and must provide for a system or interface to enable the owner of the data to modify these data.

The organization must also provide a mechanism for employees to report any suspicions they have regarding upkeep of personal data or privacy breach.

The whole objective of a data privacy governance model is to establish a framework to get together the right set of people and assign accountability to each role in order to achieve the above with the aid of policies, processes, tools, and technology. The governance model should equip the organization to monitor and prevent any privacy loss incident and provide a mechanism to handle such incidences in the case of any such occurrence.

More and more enterprises are beginning to look at a hybrid model for governance. The chief privacy officer holds the primary responsibility across the enterprise and is aided by the individual unit's privacy compliance officers, information security and risk group, incident reporting team, and steering committees for privacy protection programs. Such a hybrid model includes the right mix of centralized and decentralized or localized functions. The CIO remains the key stakeholder for any data privacy initiative.

An effective way to prevent misuse of personal information is to foster the right sensitivity toward protection of personal data among the employees. Employees must realize that they are the custodians of their customers' privacy and the governance model should influence the establishment of such a culture across the enterprise.

3

ENTERPRISE DATA CLASSIFICATION POLICY AND PRIVACY LAWS

Points to Ponder

- Why should data be classified?
- How is data classified?
- What is the basis for data classification?
- What are the privacy laws the organization must watch out for?

The existence, awareness, and implementation of the data classification policy indicate the seriousness with which an organization treats the privacy of their employees and customers. All enterprises need to be aware of the type of data/information they collect, store, process, transmit/share, and destroy or archive. In this chapter, *data* and *information* have been used interchangeably.

Different types of data need different levels of protection. For example, public data (which are all about what the organization doesn't mind the outside world knowing) need less protection as compared to say, the customer's date of birth. The objectives of any data classification policy are:

- To enable regulatory compliance
- To establish a preventive mechanism for avoidance of hefty fines in case of leakage of these data
- To assign a value to the various types of data on the basis of:
  - Tangible loss to the organization in case of leakage of this data
  - Intangible loss to the organization (such as loss of reputation to the organization) in case of leakage of this data
  - Derivative impact including loss of customers in case of leakage of this data

The challenges of data privacy regulatory compliance. (Courtesy of Jophy Joy)

Regulatory Compliance

Prior to the introduction of the data privacy protection laws, many customers/employees (or data subjects) had to bear with unsolicited promotional activities. The organizations collecting the personal data of customers misused them for targeted marketing activities although the purpose for which the personal customer data were collected was different. Once personal data have been provided to the organization, the vulnerable customer (data subject) was in the dark as to why the data were needed, how the data were being used, and which other organizations were using them, and they had no control over this. There were frequent occurrences of leakage of private data of customers and employees due to lack of appropriate protection measures.

In order to prevent this widespread menace, the European Union issued privacy protection directives to its member states to implement. The directives implemented the principles recommended by the Organization for Economic Cooperation and Development (OECD) for data privacy protection and cross-border flow of private data. These principles, also known as Fair Information Practices, essentially are about ensuring that:

- Customers (or the data subject) are aware when personal data are being collected.
- Customers (or the data subject) are aware of the purpose for which the data are being collected.

- Customers (or the data subject) are aware of the other organizations with which these data would be shared and the right of the data subject to refuse sharing these data.
- The organization collecting these data provides necessary protection against misuse and collects only as much personal data as needed and nothing extra.
- The organization provides control to the users to access and modify their personal data.
- There is a data controller who is made accountable for ensuring that the above principles are followed.

There are far too many privacy laws in the world! Tables 3.1 through 3.6 provide snapshots of various data privacy regulations relevant from a data anonymization perspective. The tables cover only the most popular or widely used privacy laws and are not a complete list of data privacy regulations.

In addition to data privacy protection, certain regulations in the United States deal with export control of sensitive defense technology

Table 3.1   PCI-DSS Act

ATTRIBUTE	DETAILS
Regulation/Standard	PCI-DSS
Description	The Payment Card Industry Data Security Standard (PCI DSS) is applicable to any business or organization handling data of Visa, Mastercard, American Express, Discover, and JCB card holders. Card here refers to debit, credit, ATM, online shopping, and POS cards.
	The standard mandates protection of the cardholder through a set of controls (12 PCI-DSS Requirements). These requirements are aimed at minimizing privacy loss and reducing identity theft with respect to cardholder data.
	Validation for compliance with these standards is performed through a security certification process. Any organization that stores, processes, or transmits card (Visa, Master, Amex, Discover, JCB) data is covered by PCI, regardless of the number of transactions per year. How the organization must verify this compliance varies according to its volume of annual card transactions.
Relevant Geography	Across the globe (wherever the writ of the payment card industry runs)
Sensitive Entity	Cardholder information.
Relevant to Industry Sector	Any industry involving cards/payments, However, the need to adhere to the PCI-DSS standards is more prevalent in the financial and retail industries.

Table 3.2   HIPAA

ATTRIBUTE	DETAILS
Regulation/Standard	HIPAA
Description	Healthcare providers in the United States need to share personal data of covered entities/medical health information of patients with insurance providers, employers, and other partners.
	Historically, the practices adopted by the healthcare providers to protect PII and PHI of the covered entities have been weak.
	In order to ensure adequate protection of PII and PHI of the covered entities as well as enable U.S. workers to continue with their existing healthcare coverage even after changing jobs, the Health Insurance Portability and Accountability Act (HIPAA) was introduced.
	This law deals with protection of PII and PHI of covered entities.
Relevant Geography	United States
Sensitive Entity	PHI (and PII)
Relevant to Industry Sector	Healthcare, insurance

Table 3.3   HITECH Act

ATTRIBUTE	DETAILS
Regulation/Standard	HITECH Act
Description	HIPAA had no enforcement power. The Health Information Technology for Economic and Clinical Health (HITECH) Act strengthens HIPAA with enforcement capabilities. The act was meant to increase the accountability and liability of the organizations associated with privacy leakage.
	The HITECH Act was aimed at encouraging healthcare organizations to switch over to electronic records
Relevant Geography	United States
Sensitive Entity	PHI
Relevant to Industry Sector	Healthcare, insurance

such as ITAR. Even for these laws, data anonymization is a relevant mechanism for sensitive data protection.

There are various other laws and statutes that are related to privacy in one way or another including FERPA, COPPA, FCRA, and DPPA, which are very specific to protection of privacy of students, families, or drivers or are applicable to credit rating agencies. There are also data privacy acts such as the Cable Communications Policy Act (CCPA) which is meant to protect the privacy (personal data) of the customers of cable service providers. In addition, there are several state-level privacy laws. Not all these regulations may be applicable

Table 3.4 GLBA

ATTRIBUTE	DETAILS
Regulation/Standard	GLBA
Description	The primary objective of the Gramm–Leach–Bliley Act (GLBA) is to remove hurdles for those businesses wanting to create a financial supermarket by providing investment banking, retail banking, and insurance services to consumers.
	Prior to this act, consolidation of investment bank, retail bank, and insurance company was prohibited. This rule defines the "consumer" as an individual who buys any of the financial products of the business/financial institution and mandates strong financial privacy protection of personal data of this consumer.
	The key elements of financial privacy include most of the standard OECD principles, that is:
	• Informing the consumer about the purpose for which the consumer's personal information is being collected, where the information is being used and with whom it is being shared
	• Informing the consumer on the measures being adopted for protecting his or her personal information
	• In the case where the consumer is not interested in the sharing of his or her personal information with any of the parties, the consumer must have a right to opt out.
Relevant Geography	United States
Sensitive Entity	Consumer PII/Consumer Financial Information
Relevant to Industry Sector	Banking, financial institution, insurance

Table 3.5 PIPEDA

ATTRIBUTE	DETAILS
Regulation/Standard	PIPEDA
Description	Personal Information Protection and Electronic Documents Act (PIPEDA) deals with the protection provided to personal information during the collection, transmission, processing, and storage of this information by private organizations.
	Most of the provinces in Canada have derivative laws including the Personal Information Protection Act (British Columbia) and Personal Health Information Protection Act (Ontario).
Relevant Geography	Canada
Sensitive Entity	PII
Relevant to Industry Sector	Private sector organizations

Table 3.6   European Data Protection Directive

ATTRIBUTE	DETAILS
Regulation/Standard	European Data Protection Directive
Description	The European Data Protection directive is intended to regulate processing of personal information, facilitate introduction of standard privacy laws across all of Europe, and enable free flow of data across the European Union with high levels of protection being provided to personal data.
	These directives implemented the OECD data protection principles such as directing organizations to collect only as much personal information is needed, being transparent to the customer (data subject) on why (purpose) the data are needed, with whom the data will be shared, and what the measures are for protecting the personal data.
	The European Data Protection Directive resulted in most member states as well as the United Kingdom formulating their data protection acts and establishing an information commissioner/privacy commissioner office for regulating the use of personal data. Most of the above acts made it mandatory for any organization collecting or processing personal data to register with these commissioners.
Relevant Geography	Europe
Sensitive Entity	PII
Relevant to Industry Sector	Any organization dealing with PII

to your organization and the legal department would be helpful in identifying their relevance to the enterprise.

Enterprise Data Classification

The typical enterprise data classification categories or levels in ascending order of privacy level would be:

Shareable without any restrictions: If there is no reason for restricting this data being accessed by anyone inside or outside the enterprise, this data can be classified as *shareable* or *public*. Examples of such information include the organization name, head office addresses, stock price, and the like.

Shareable with restrictions: If this information is necessary to be known by internal employees (and potentially contractors) but should not be made available to the external world without due authorization, then it is classified as *shareable with*

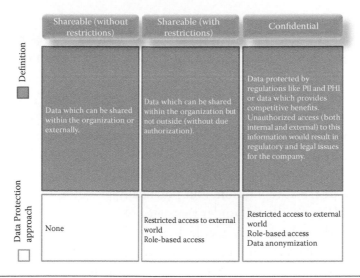

Figure 3.1 Enterprise data classification snapshot.

restrictions or *internal*. Policy data on employee compensation benefits or leaves can belong to this category.

Confidential: This is essentially the data that should not be shared inside or outside the enterprise and must be protected due to the competitive benefits it provides or regulatory nature of this data.

Figure 3.1 depicts a snapshot of the enterprise data classification along with their corresponding approach for protection.

SUBCLASSIFICATION OF CONFIDENTIAL DATA

Confidential data are further classified in different ways by different organization like:

1. *Client Confidential* data and *Corporate Confidential* data
2. *Restricted* data and *Regulated* data
3. *Restricted* data, *Regulated* data and *Top Secret* or *Highly Confidential* data

Corporate Confidential data or *Restricted* data are made available only to authorized internal users, contractors, partners, and vendors, and not made available to unauthorized users as it may impact the organizational effectiveness or competitive edge of the organization. Typically, the impact of leakage of a restricted category of data can be managed without any adverse impact to the enterprise. Projects specific data is an example of *Corporate Confidential* data or *Restricted* data.

Client Confidential data or *Regulated* data are protected with a high level of security as leakage of this category of data would lead to hefty fines due to noncompliance to privacy regulations. The other adverse impact of leakage of this category of data could be loss of trust, reputation, and potentially loss of business. PII and PHI generally fall under this category.

In order to specially tackle high business impact information breaches, some organizations have another category or class called *Top Secret* or *Highly Confidential*. This is the category of data needing the highest level of security and privacy protection.

Points to Consider

- The higher the privacy level is, the higher the protection needed.
- The data privacy guidelines of most organizations mandate that data belonging to highest privacy level(s) should be anonymized or encrypted.
- There can be cases where the classification of data may change from one category to another over a period of time. For example, valuation of the company planned for takeover by the enterprise may be confidential before the actual announcement of the M&A (merger and acquisition), but may become public once the announcement is made.

Controls for Each Class of Enterprise Data

In this context, controls can be viewed as a set of protection measures applied to prevent or eliminate an identified privacy and security risk. These controls are applied when data are collected, transmitted, distributed, shared, stored, and disposed of. In the case of documents, controls (labeling) also ensure that the document reader is aware of the class or category of information held by the document. Table 3.7 provides an overview of the various controls.

Table 3.7 Controls Applied for Each Class of Data

CLASS OF ENTERPRISE DATA	CONTROLS
Shareable (without restrictions)	• No controls
Shareable (with restrictions)	• External access prevention • Role-based permissions
Regulated/Confidential	• External access prevention • Role-based permissions • Encryption and/or data anonymization of data at rest • Encryption of data in motion

Conclusion

Every organization needs to know the type of data it deals with and must be able to differentiate between the important data, the sensitive data, and the not-so sensitive data it handles and must have separate policies and controls for them. The enterprise data classification policy is a means to achieve the above. The objectives of any data classification policy are:

- To facilitate compliance with various privacy laws.
- To establish a preventive mechanism for avoidance of hefty fines in the case of leakage of these data.
- Assign a value to the different types of data on the basis of various parameters such as direct and derivative loss to the organization in case of misuse or leakage.

The typical privacy laws we come across before embarking on any data privacy protection initiative such as data anonymization include PCI-DSS, HIPAA, European Data Privacy Directives, GLBA, PIPEDA, and HITECH Act. There are other privacy laws that are specific to the industry or geography and the legal department needs to be on board for identifying the laws applicable to the enterprise.

In ascending order of privacy levels, the typical data classes are shareable (with and without restrictions) and confidential. The higher the privacy or sensitivity level is, the higher the protection and security needed to handle these data. The controls vary as per the sensitivity level. In most organizations, data anonymization is one of the key measures used for prevention of misuse of confidential data.

4

OPERATIONAL PROCESSES, GUIDELINES, AND CONTROLS FOR ENTERPRISE DATA PRIVACY PROTECTION

Points to Ponder

- What are the operational processes, guidelines, and controls to be implemented for data privacy protection?
- What are the objectives of privacy incident management?
- How should privacy incidents that have escaped the net of preventive controls be handled?
- What is a privacy incident response plan? What are its key components?

In order to have an efficient data privacy protection system, the organization needs to bring together policies, controls, and procedures. These need to be supported by awareness programs, training programs, and effective incident handling procedures.

In this chapter, we get to see how the ecosystem of enterprisewide data Privacy policies, guidelines, and processes needs to complement data anonymization in order to achieve the objectives of data anonymization, i.e., protect against misuse of data, which the enterprise considers as sensitive.

As in the previous chapters, *data* and *information* have been used interchangeably in this chapter. Similarly, "data privacy incident," "privacy incident," and "incident" are used interchangeably throughout this chapter. The same holds true for "privacy" and "data privacy."

The enterprise data privacy policies specify in generic terms:

- What should be treated as PII by the organization?
- What should be treated as PHI by the organization?
- Who can access PII/PHI?

Guidelines for enterprise privacy data protection. (Courtesy of Jophy Joy)

- How is PII/PHI supposed to be handled as part of any daily transactions?
- What are the protection mechanisms to be used when collecting, storing, and transmitting PII/PHI?
- How should PII/PHI be retained, archived, or destroyed?
- How should PII/PHI be handled as part of a software development life cycle?
- How should any PII/PHI breach incident be reported? Who should report it? How should the incident be handled?
- What are the penal actions that would be taken in the case of violation of these policies or nonadherence to policies?[1]

Policies are enforced by controls. Controls are the countermeasures used to tackle any privacy issue, incident, or event that affects the organization in a negative manner. In this section, privacy event, privacy issue, and privacy incident have been used synonymously. They all affect the organization negatively.

A large subset of the information security controls and measures, as noted in the *Official (ISC)2 Guide to the CISSPR CBKR*, can also be extended to the data privacy arena. Table 4.1 depicts the different types of controls along with examples These control types can be either manual or automatic or a combination of both.

These controls are enforced through:

- *Separation of Responsibilities:* A user having access to anonymized data will not have access to original (or identifiable) data.

Table 4.1   Types of Privacy Controls[3]

PRIVACY CONTROL TYPE	DESCRIPTION	EXAMPLE OF A PRIVACY CONTROL
Preventive	These are controls that seek to prevent any privacy event/issue/incident that affects the organization in a negative manner from happening	Access controls Data anonymization Encryption
Detective	Not all events can be predicted. Preventive controls mostly address attacks from known sources. Attacks from unknown sources generally pass through preventive controls Thus detective controls are those that help identify details about the privacy incident after it has occurred or when it occurs	Audit logs Periodic assessments, reviews Tests
Corrective	These are controls that minimize the impact of the event after it has occurred and intend to prevent the incident from recurring	Policies Privacy incident handling Awareness sessions Privacy training
Recovery	These are controls that enable the organization (affected information system) to return to normal or steady state after the occurrence of an event	Privacy incident handling procedures Business continuity and disaster recovery procedures
Directive	These are administrative or legal in nature and mandate compliance. These are controls that wield the stick of hefty fines or prosecution in case of violation of directives	Privacy regulations Policies and guidelines Agreement

This will prevent the user from tracing or reconstructing the original data and potentially misusing them.

- *Role-Based Access Control and Remote Access Restrictions*: Access to PII/PHI is restricted from both a role perspective as well as location perspective. Different roles have different levels (read/write/modify) of access to PII/PHI. Remote access locations to PII/PHI are restricted.
- *Least Privilege*: Normal users will not have system admin privileges and only the least privilege will be provided in terms of access. This can be, say, read access to the tables.
- *Need to Know*: No internal staffer will be allowed access unless the lack of access prevents the staffer from discharging assigned duties.

MEDIA ACCESS, STORAGE, AND DESTRUCTION POLICIES[1]

PII/PHI can reside as digital information on CD-ROMs, tapes, and the like, or in nondigital forms such as paper or films. Most organizations have security procedures and guidelines associated with both formats. For sensitive PII/PHI stored on paper, the guidelines talk about shredding paper before disposal. For digital formats, the controls are:

- To label the digital media with appropriate labels to denote the appropriate level of information classification.
- To store and transmit PII/PHI in an encrypted format.
- To sanitize the media from PII/PHI before destruction or disposal of the media.
- To restrict PII/PHI from being stored on portable devices such as USB Flash drives or mobile phones.

- *Periodic Reviews of Any Unauthorized Access*: Periodic reviews provide a hint of any unauthorized access to PII/PHI so that corrective action can be taken and mischief mongers can be identified for taking action.
- *Encryption of PII/PHI When Being Backed Up*: Data backups are typically done on hard drives, or backup tapes. PII/PHI is typically stored in an encrypted format here. Controls around disposal of such media include sanitization of storage from PII/PHI before disposal or destruction.
- *Contracts with Partners*: Contracts and agreements are signed to ensure that any third party (partners, contracting agencies, consultants) dealing with PII/PHI will need to follow organizational PII/PHI protection policies.

Figure 4.1 provides a snapshot of controls for handling PII/PHI. These controls need to be complemented with regular employee awareness sessions or mailers on PII/PHI protection, mandatory privacy training sessions, periodic privacy assessments and audits, security audit logs, and usage of data loss prevention tools to observe unusual activities.

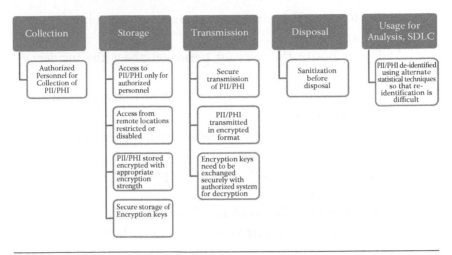

Figure 4.1 PII/PHI control snapshot.

PRIVACY TRAINING

The objective of training programs should be to enable staff to identify what PII is, what PHI is, and to realize when they are dealing with PII/PHI and how to deal with PII/PHI. The training must also enable staff to identify when there is a misuse of PII/PHI and encourage them to report any misuse.

Privacy Incident Management

Despite all the preventive mechanisms in place, there is still the possibility of misuse, wrongful disclosure, or destruction of sensitive data. Dealing with such privacy incidents requires the organization to be prepared in terms of handling the impact of the incident within a short timeframe. This calls for a mature privacy incident handling process aided by usage of appropriate people and tools. The better the preparedness of the organization is, the smaller the timeframe needed to resolve the incident and the smaller the negative impact on the business.

Privacy incident management is the:

- Ability of the enterprise to spot privacy incidents quickly by enabling reporting of the incident by means of a common portal or a helpdesk

- Ability to classify the incidents as per severity and impact on the enterprise
- Ability to notify the relevant personnel about the incident (preferably as part of an automated workflow)
- Ability to isolate high-severity incidents within a short timeframe by means of tools
- Existence of appropriate processes for handling incidences of different severity
- Existence of policies and processes to prosecute the mischief maker legally
- Ability to analyze the incident, identify the root cause of the incident, and prevent further occurrences of the incident

Not every issue needs to be dealt with in the same manner and be resolved within the same timeframe. The incidents can be classified based on the severity which in turn can be based on the negative impact the incident has on the organization.

The severity of an incident can be based on the:

- Quantity of records affected or compromised
- Violation of regulations and hefty fines imposed by the regulator for noncompliance
- Impact on business
- Potential reputation loss or loss of customers
- Potential loss of business
- Financial impact

Table 4.2 shows a sample privacy incident severity matrix.

Planning for Incident Resolution

Incident resolution plans must equip the incident response team for handling the following stages:[2]

- Preparation
- Incident capture
- Incident response and
- Post incident activities

Table 4.2   Privacy Incident Severity Matrix

	LOW SEVERITY	MEDIUM SEVERITY	HIGH SEVERITY
Quantity of records compromised	Few	Good number	High number
Tangible loss	Low	Medium (e.g., some customers are concerned and some customers are planning to leave)	High (e.g., loss of customers)
Intangible loss	Low	Medium (potential negative publicity)	High (loss of reputation)
Regulatory impact	Warnings issued by regulatory authority	Small fine imposed	Lawsuits by affected customers Withdrawal of license to engage in business
Example	Small number of customers or staff members are receiving marketing materials or cold calls from the company for products for which customers or staff have not subscribed	Small number of staff PII/PHI suspected to have been compromised	Large number of customer PII/PHI compromised
SLAs	<10 days	<20 days	<30 days
Personnel involved in incident management in addition to chief privacy officer and unit/department privacy officers	Information security and risk personnel, department head	Senior management, department head, senior personnel from information security and risk department, legal department, public relations officer	Head of the organization, senior management, department head, chief information security and risk officer, legal department, public relations officer

Preparation

The ability of the organization to respond to any privacy incident and resolve the incident quickly thereby minimizing the impact of the incident is wholly dependent on how well prepared the organization is. Preparation involves the:

- Formulation of privacy policies and defined processes for handling different incidents of varying levels of severity

- Acquisition of the ability to classify the incidents into different severity levels
- Awareness of (as well as defined procedures on) who is to be notified for what type of incidents and when to involve the legal team
- Availability of tools and technology to identify the cause of the incident
- Awareness of (as well as defined procedures on) how and when to report to the media, affected staff, or customers about occurrence of incident as well as who should report this
- Awareness of (as well as defined procedures on) how and when to report to the regulatory authorities
- Awareness of what PII/PHI is and what constitutes a case of misuse across the organization through awareness and training programs
- Availability of a mechanism for staff to report suspicious privacy incidents

Incident Capture

This involves capturing the following details (in a database) when a privacy incident is reported:

- *What* is the incident?
- *When* was the incident observed?
- *Who* has reported the incident?
- *Who* has discovered the incident?
- *What* is the extent of the incident, and so on?

The key components for capturing incidents would be:

- Accessible portals, website, hotlines, or helpdesks to enable staff to report misuse of PII/PHI
- Database to record the event details
- Notification system
- Optionally, an automated workflow system to trigger notifications once an incident is reported

The key components along with the incident detail captures should enable the privacy incident monitoring team to classify the incident into severity level and notify the relevant response team members and stakeholders.

Incident Response

Incident response involves detection of unauthorized access, security log analysis, audit log analysis, determination of the impact of the incident, and notification of appropriate personnel (including legal teams). The objective of any incident response team is to isolate the source of the incident, minimize the negative impact of the incident, and wherever possible, eradicate the incident. Wherever there has been a loss of PII/PHI, they may need to be restored from backups.

High-severity incidents would require establishment of close coordination channels between various stakeholders including the legal team, chief security/privacy officers, CIO, and corporate communications. Any PII/PHI compromise or loss may have to be communicated to affected customers by the managers responsible for the customer accounts and a potential grievance redressing mechanism may have to be provided for these customers. Legal representatives may also have to file reports to the regulatory authorities. Media would have to be engaged carefully to ensure that there is no miscommunication of the impact.

The key components for incidence response would be:

- Data loss prevention systems/intrusion detection systems
- Security testing tools
- PII/PHI audit monitoring tools
- Security log analysis mechanisms

Post Incident Analysis

The objective of this phase is to identify the root cause of the incident by performing a detailed analysis from the available logs and taking steps to forestall recurrence of the event. This might imply the updating of privacy incident handling policies and processes as well as systems. The key component here is the usage of various analysis and reporting tools.

Figure 4.2 depicts the multiple stages any privacy incident response plan must handle. In many organizations; the privacy incident

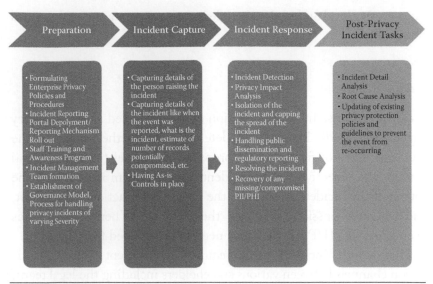

Figure 4.2   Privacy incident response plan.

response team is a subset of the information security incident response team. The whole function of data privacy management itself is connected to information security and risk management for administrative purposes.

Guidelines and Best Practices

Enterprise privacy guidelines are aids to performing daily tasks associated with PII/PHI. The following sections make up a typical list of privacy guidelines and best practices.[1,3]

PII/PHI Collection Guidelines

- Any authorized personnel collecting PII/PHI must state the purpose of collecting the PII/PHI to the individual and obtain consent of the individual for the PII/PHI being used for the purpose. The personnel must also inform the individual of the protection measures adopted by the organization to protect PII/PHI.
- Online information systems collecting PII/PHI must
  - State the purpose of collecting the PII/PHI by providing a website link to the privacy policies of the organization.

This website link must list the PII/PHI protection measures adopted by the organization.

- Provide a mechanism to obtain the consent of the individual for storing PII/PHI.
- Provide a mechanism to ensure accuracy of the PII/PHI by providing a link for the individual to update PII/PHI.
- Provide a mechanism for the individual to deny consent for usage of PII/PHI (unless mandated by legalities).

Guidelines for Storage and Transmission of PII/PHI

- Only as much PII/PHI as needed for running the business and nothing additional may be stored.
- PII/PHI should not be stored in as-is format in production systems and ideally should be encrypted with an appropriate level of strength which ensures that PII/PHI is not compromised. The keys for decryption should be stored in a protected store and must be access-controlled. Only authorized users should have access to keys for decryption.
- The keys used for encryption should be refreshed periodically.
- When PII/PHI needs to be transmitted to another system, it should be transmitted securely in an encrypted format.
- Wherever the receiving system wants access to the key for decryption, the keys should be exchanged through a secure infrastructure.
- Keys should be backed up to ensure that authorized users have a way to get back original PII/PHI.

PII/PHI Usage Guidelines

Typically activities such as application development, testing, and statistical analysis need more realistic personal data with the relationship with other data elements being preserved. Here we may not be able to use encryption and need to use alternate de-identification techniques or algorithms. For such cases, the controls must ensure that the data cannot be reidentified or can be reidentified only by authorized people. In these cases, the reidentification techniques or algorithms must not be available to the user accessing the anonymized data. Separation of responsibilities, wherein the same person must not have access to both deanonymized and anonymized data, must be enforced.

Guidelines for Storing PII/PHI on Portable Devices and Storage Devices

Typically PII/PHI must not be allowed to be stored on portable devices. If absolutely necessary, they must be encrypted and stored. Any encryption keys must also be secured.

Guidelines for Staff

- Privacy training must be conducted periodically, employees must attend the sessions, and there must be mandatory certification.
- Personal data must be treated with care.
- PII/PHI may be transmitted outside the enterprise network only after encryption.
- Any suspicious incident or suspicious coworker behavior must be reported immediately through the privacy/security incident portal.

The organization, on its part, must enable staff to report any privacy misuse or theft by providing access to a common portal or helpdesk, which in turn can trigger the appropriate next steps for dealing with the incident in an automated manner. All the above operational processes, guidelines, and controls hold good for any other highly competitive, sensitive, or regulated information that the organization may handle in addition to PII and PHI.

Conclusion

In order to ensure the success of privacy protection initiatives, data anonymization implementation needs to be accompanied by other mechanisms such as the establishment of operational controls, procedures, and information privacy policies.

Preventive mechanisms can exist only for known privacy abuses. For unexpected privacy issues, an efficient incident response plan and grievance redressal mechanism needs to be in place in order to minimize the negative impact of PII/PHI leakage or theft.

Privacy incidents are of different severity. The incident response mechanism must ensure that the severity of the incident can be determined based on established criteria and the response processes are different for different levels of severity.

References

1. NIST (Guide to Protecting the Confidentiality of Personally Identifiable Information) (Special Publication 800-122).
2. NIST SP 800-61.
3. Official (ISC)2 Guide to the CISSPR CBKR.

5

The Different Phases of a Data Anonymization Program

Points to Ponder

- What are the activities involved in an end-to-end enterprise-wide data anonymization program and which are the activities where the project sponsor needs to get involved?
- Why should the organization invest in data anonymization implementation?
- If data anonymization can be implemented using SQL encryption scripts, why should the organization go for an anonymization tool?
- When can a data anonymization program be termed successful?

Senior management buy-in and planning are important stepping stones to the success of a data anonymization program.* We look at data anonymization from a project sponsor's perspective in this chapter and discuss how to get management to buy into the enterprise data anonymization program implementation as well as how to plan and execute the implementation. As in the previous chapters, "data privacy" and "privacy" have been used interchangeably in this chapter.

How Should I Go about the Enterprise Data Anonymization Program?

Misuse of personal data is an enterprisewide issue and any assessment of the as-is data practices should be taken up across the enterprise. An end-to-end anonymization program can be phased out as shown in Figure 5.1.

---

* In this chapter, *program* is used to indicate a time-bound initiative. The usage of the word *program* does not imply a computer program, unless explicitly mentioned as "computer program."

Is this your management's attitude toward data anonymization programs? (Courtesy of Jophy Joy)

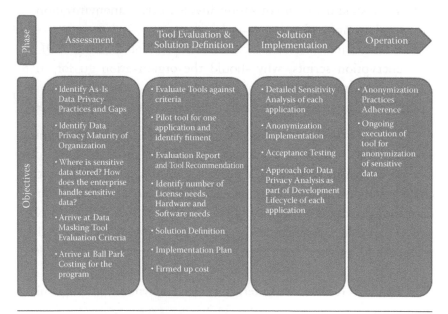

Phase	Assessment	Tool Evaluation & Solution Definition	Solution Implementation	Operation
Objectives	• Identify As-Is Data Privacy Practices and Gaps • Identify Data Privacy Maturity of Organization • Where is sensitive data stored? How does the enterprise handle sensitive data? • Arrive at Data Masking Tool Evaluation Criteria • Arrive at Ball Park Costing for the program	• Evaluate Tools against criteria • Pilot tool for one application and identify fitment • Evaluation Report and Tool Recommendation • Identify number of License needs, Hardware and Software needs • Solution Definition • Implementation Plan • Firmed up cost	• Detailed Sensitivity Analysis of each application • Anonymization Implementation • Acceptance Testing • Approach for Data Privacy Analysis as part of Development Lifecycle of each application	• Anonymization Practices Adherence • Ongoing execution of tool for anonymization of sensitive data

Figure 5.1   End-to-end enterprise data anonymization lifecycle.

The Assessment Phase

This phase can be termed as the prerequisite for planning out any data anonymization implementation.

Given that a number of stakeholders such as application owners, business analysts, DBAs, and system administrators across the enterprise

along with the legal team and the information security and risk department personnel need to be interviewed to understand the as-is practices
and attitude with respect to data privacy protection, it is better to have
external consultants with expertise in data privacy and information privacy execute the assessment phase and come out with a detailed report
along with recommendations.

   As part of this phase, the following are the questions that need to
be discussed and answered before embarking on an enterprisewide
data anonymization program:

- Which department owns data privacy in the organization?
- What are the laws the organization is bound by in each coun-
  try and state?
- How do I get my legal team to help support the data anony-
  mization initiative?
- Who should be part of the steering committee for privacy?
- Who will fund this program?
- What are the as-is data practices in my organization?
- Is there any policy with respect to handling sensitive data?
  How is data classified in the organization? Is there a policy
  for classifying these data?
- What are the data privacy-related gaps in the enterprise?
- Have any known data privacy issues been encountered? How
  were they solved earlier?
- At what level of maturity is my organization with respect to
  handling data privacy-related issues?
- Where are the sensitive data stored?
- Which tool should be used for anonymization? What are the
  existing tools used for data anonymization?
- What are the criteria for evaluation of the tool?
- How decentralized should this program be? Should each
  department be allowed to use its own tool?
- What should be the timeframe for completion of the data
  anonymization program?
- What will the overall cost look like?
- How do I get senior management buy-in?
- What will the governance be for monitoring this program?
  Who will be accountable for what activity?

- Should third-party consultants be engaged for the implementation? Are there any laws restricting the involvement of consultants who are not citizens of the country?
- Who will certify the implementation?
- What processes need to be taken as follow-up to ensure that employees and contractors comply with privacy regulations and take this process forward?
- Who will ensure maintenance of the solution and any operational activity arising out of the implementation?

At the end of this phase, we will get an order of magnitude of the data anonymization implementation effort and budget required for this program.

Tool Evaluation and Solution Definition Phase

Based on the criteria arrived at as part of the assessment phase, we look at which data masking tool on the market is a good fit for the organization. Obviously, the assessment phase would have narrowed down the list to two or three vendors. These tools would be evaluated on sample representative applications to choose the right tool for the enterprise. The popular vendors of data anonymization tools are provided in a subsequent chapter in this book.

This phase can further look at the scope of the data anonymization implementation and document the approach for data anonymization using the tool. The solution and approach to anonymize data across various technologies and formats leveraging the tool and using anonymized data for important integration scenarios can be taken up for definition. At the end of this phase, a firmed-up cost including operational costs and a detailed plan for data anonymization implementation should be made available.

Data Anonymization Implementation Phase

This phase involves identifying the sensitive fields as per data privacy guidelines of the enterprise for each application in scope. The best fit standardized technique for anonymization can be chosen. Any customization of the tool is also executed by the vendor during this phase and the anonymization solution is implemented.

The applications can be anonymized based on priority and a phased approach across departments helps in better change management than does a big bang approach. The amount of effort for implementation of data anonymization depends on various parameters including the number of fields to be anonymized, and number of tables, files, and other data stores such as message queues to be analyzed and scoped for this exercise.

Application architects, business analysts, data modelers/designers, and application owners would be interviewed for understanding application architecture, integration architecture, data flow, and business processes where sensitive data are handled during the sensitive analysis phase.

The IT service vendors supported by the application team would be involved in implementation of anonymization for the applications. They perform the sensitivity analysis, the anonymization design activities such as choosing the appropriate anonymization technique for the sensitive fields, and execution of the anonymization scripts, whereas the application testers will be involved in the final stages of validating and certifying that the application behaves unchanged with anonymized data. Care should be taken to ensure that these application testers are not able to trace back the original value.

The other activities include the setup of hardware and software infrastructure needed for the anonymization environment. DBAs and system administrators may also need to be involved for access to environment and data stores. By the end of this phase, the approach to continued adherence to the anonymization process must be clear to the employees or contractors who will be maintaining the application. The process for movement of data from production to nonproduction environments must be well established.

Operations Phase or the Steady-State Phase

This phase comprises activities after the implementation of anonymization for the application. Typical activities include anonymization of sensitive data whenever fresh data dumps are needed from the production environment for testing application upgrades and fixes.

The application developers need to have a data sensitivity analysis or data privacy analysis process embedded in the software enhancement/maintenance life cycle. Anonymization scripts must be updated when any new sensitive field is introduced or any existing sensitive field is removed as part of application upgrades and fixes. The anonymization scripts can be versioned, if necessary. The tool plays an important role in the anonymization process adherence. How seamlessly the tool integrates with the as-is data flow processes in the enterprise decides the ease of absorption of the data anonymization process into the operational procedures.

Food for Thought

As an enterprise anonymization project sponsor, the following sections give some of the preparatory questions for which we need to have answers.

When Should the Organization Invest in a Data Anonymization Exercise?

A simple rule of thumb here is if the organization collects, stores, processes, and exchanges PII or PHI of customers and employees and there is no sensitivity shown by the employees in handling these data and they have access to these data in their original form, the organization is sitting on a time bomb. It is just a matter of time before an incident of a misuse of personal data (of customers, employees, or partners) occurs. It is always better to have data anonymization before the first incident of such nature occurs.

The Organization's Security Policies Mandate Authorization to Be Built into Every Application. Won't this Be Sufficient? Why is Data Anonymization Needed?

Most people confuse data security with data privacy protection. Data privacy protection is preventing the unintended use of personal data whereas data security is about protecting the CIA (confidentiality, integrity, and availability) aspects of data. Misuse of data can be the intent behind a data theft or the outcome of a data theft.

Data theft can be prevented by handling the CIA aspects of data. Authorization and access control along with physical and network security can help prevent data theft. Data anonymization is meant to solve the problem of sensitive data being made available for testers and application developers. Table 5.1 shows the difference between data authorization and data anonymization.

Table 5.1 Difference Between Data Authorization and Data Anonymization

	DATA ANONYMIZATION	DATA AUTHORIZATION
Details	Data anonymization hides the original data by transforming their value and ensures that even if an unauthorized user gets hold of these data, they are of no use as the original value of the data cannot be traced back. This technique falls in the realm of data privacy preservation.	Data authorization is about preventing access to original data. It falls in the realm of data security rather than data privacy preservation.
Environment	Data anonymization is relevant to nonproduction environments and can also be used in production environments for process support and technical support activities.	Data authorization is primarily concerned with the production environment.
Implementation	Data anonymization can be implemented by either using SQL scripts for encryption of sensitive data or data masking tools that leverage various data anonymization techniques and algorithms.	Data authorization can be implemented using identity management tools or custom authorization applications.

Is There a Business Case for a Data Anonymization Program in My Organization?

If the organization handles or stores customer or employee PII or PHI and needs to use these data across environments or transmit these data to vendors or partners, the case for data anonymization is a loud YES. What is the right amount of investment needed for this program is the call we need to make.

On a broad level, the total cost of a data anonymization program is made up of:

- Governance costs
- Data masking tool licensing cost
- Data anonymization implementation cost
- Operational and infrastructure cost

The *assessment* phase can help us arrive at the extent of the data anonymization required for the enterprise and also help us arrive at an approximate cost and effort needed for governance, data-masking-tool licensing, solution implementation, and operations, and thereby help build a business case. The details of the assessment exercise have already been provided in an earlier section in this chapter.

Taking the Ponemon Institute's estimation of the average cost of the loss of one record containing sensitive data as $214,[1] the *saved losses* by data anonymization can be calculated by multiplying this value with the number of customer and employee records being handled or stored. Ponemon Institute mentions that the approximate cost of $214 per record leaked takes care of both the tangible and intangible costs such as loss of reputation.

Based on the assessment exercise and the calculated *saved losses* or *prevented cost*, we can look at a rough order of magnitude of investment and scope that would justify the investment. For example, as part of the assessment exercise, if we find that most applications in a portfolio are rarely tested (and not tested in an integration test environment), handle minimal sensitive data, and already use SQL encryption scripts for anonymizing data, there is no need to re-implement data anony-mization using a data masking tool again for these applications. We can continue to live with the existing SQL encryption scripts. There is no business case for a data masking tool implementation for this port-folio unless the parameters change, i.e., the applications are frequently modified and/or used in an integration test where the integration files also contain sensitive data.

When Can a Data Anonymization Program Be Called a Successful One?

One of the parameters to identify the success of data anonymization implementation is a reduction in the number of incidents of personal data misuse due to insiders. However, if there were no documented incidents of personal data misuse prior to the implementation of data anonymization, this may not be a convincing argument for proclaim-ing its success.

Success of the data anonymization program can be based on a mix of the following outcomes:

- Voluntary and rigorous adoption of data anonymization guidelines and procedures by employees
- High commitment level shown by the employees to preserve privacy of sensitive customer and employee data

- Extent of the adoption of data anonymization across the enterprise
- Usage of anonymized data for integration testing and other IT application development activities
- Unmasked sensitive data being available only to a few authorized personnel in the organization
- Integration of data privacy and sensitivity analysis with the organization's software development life cycle

Why Should I Go for a Data Anonymization Tool When SQL Encryption Scripts Can Be Used to Anonymize Data?

Even (database column-level) encryption using SQL scripts is a valid approach for data anonymization. This is a simplistic approach especially when you have the same database technology across the enterprise. The problem with this approach arises when you have different technologies for databases and you need to perform an integration test of these applications.

Challenges with Using the SQL Encryption Scripts Approach for Data Anonymization

- When native-SQL is used to encrypt the sensitive data belonging to different databases, the value generated for the same input is not the same in each of the databases. For example, the same customer would appear as different customers in each database and an integration test is almost impossible in such a scenario.
- Even when the same database technology is widespread across the enterprise, there are issues with taking the SQL encryption scripts route especially with respect to scalability. SQL encryption is heavily developer dependent. Any upgrading of a database needs a rewrite of the SQL scripts. Any change to the schema needs a rewrite and the question of who will maintain the scripts on an on-going basis comes up and what if the developer quits the organization!
- Given that the code is highly customized to each application, the issue of standardization across the enterprises comes into

the picture. What if the applications belonging to different departments need to integrate? Should the code (SQL encryption scripts) be rewritten? And what if different departments are on different versions of the same technology; should the department with the older version upgrade to a newer version?

- Testers don't like encrypted data. In most enterprises, even if use of SQL-encrypted data is mandated for nonproduction environments, the acceptance testers (who are largely business users of the application) take an exception approval for using the data without anonymization for their testing activities.
- Most of the applications need to process feed files. How to use files for testing if the database is anonymized using SQL encryption techniques is another issue.

All these challenges increase the effort, time, and cost of the application development life cycle even for minor releases or upgrades forcing enterprises to take a deeper look at alternatives. Comparatively, leveraging data masking tools helps improve productivity and scalability when anonymizing data and supports a wide variety of anonymization techniques in addition to cryptographic techniques. Hence, for any enterprisewide data anonymization initiative, it is better to go in for data masking tools rather than SQL encryption scripts.

What Are the Benefits Provided by Data Masking Tools for Data Anonymization?

Data masking tools help standardize the data anonymization approach. They come with out-of-the-box support for standard data formats and multiple techniques for data anonymization. These tools help in leveraging "realistic data" for testing and reduce the effort and time needed for rewrite of the anonymization script for any application upgrades.

Why Is a Tool Evaluation Phase Needed?

There are different types of vendors on the market. There are niche vendors who support only data masking and there are vendors who support data masking as part of a larger suite of a test data management package.

Not all the tools on the market support the various technologies and file formats in the enterprise. Thus the evaluation phase is needed for identifying the best fit for your enterprise needs. It is advisable to go in for a pilot phase of evaluation where one or two integration testing scenarios can be tested using the anonymized data from the tool.

The license price of the data masking tools is also not very transparent. Most vendors provide a standard quote with the assumption that there will be no customization needed for the enterprise. Once you sign up with them, they start talking about how your enterprise systems are much different from the world's and impress upon you the need to cough up additional customization fees, which ends up increasing the cost of your overall data anonymization implementation. The evaluation phase helps you iron out these issues.

Who Should Implement Data Anonymization? Should It Be the Tool Vendor, the IT Service Partner, External Consultants, or Internal Employees?

This needs to be a carefully thought-out decision and the answer to this question varies based on how tightly regulated your industry is. Highly regulated industries such as defense companies mandate that those implementing data anonymization should be different from the tool vendor as well as the employees. The reason behind this mandate is to ensure that those who will need to use the anonymized data must not be able to trace back the original data. Thus, the anonymization tool vendor not being allowed to implement data anonymization eliminates the risk of the tool vendor using techniques that can trace back the anonymized data.

Highly regulated industries such as defense also place restrictions on "who can perform data anonymization" and these regulations vary by country. Many defense companies mandate that only citizens of that country should have access to unmasked data and should perform anonymization of the data. Separation of responsibilities is the key concern here. Internal employees are needed to facilitate approvals and sign-offs and may also be part of the testing team.

Other industries including banking, financial services, insurance, and healthcare services use a mix of vendors, IT service partners, and employees for different activities at different stages of the implementation. Tool vendors are used to install and configure the tool and train the IT service vendors and employees who later may be involved in data anonymization implementation and consultation activities. They may also be consulted for best practices and in case of any performance issues.

How Many Rounds of Testing Must Be Planned to Certify That Application Behavior Is Unchanged with Use of Anonymized Data?

This question is important to ensure availability of application testers for the anonymization initiative.

At least two rounds of testing of the application with anonymized data are needed to ensure this certification. In the case of any change of behavior, a call needs to be made on an alternate approach that may need the involvement of multiple stakeholders. Although in most cases use of a different anonymization technique may solve this issue, there may be a need to leave one or several fields unanonymized. A decision on this can involve discussions with multiple stakeholders. Usually if the sensitivity level associated with the field is lower, that is, the risk of having these data revealed is not high (cost impact is not high), we can go ahead with the decision to leave this field unmasked. Otherwise, an alternate technique needs to be found by the vendor.

Conclusion

From a data anonymization program sponsor perspective, an end-to-end data anonymization program consists of four broad phases:

Assessment Phase: Provides an understanding of where the enterprise is with respect to data privacy protection and a rough order estimate of the cost.

Anonymization Tool Evaluation and Solution Definition Phase: Helps in choosing the tool after a detailed evaluation, provides a high-level anonymization solution leveraging the tool, and provides a detailed estimate of the costs and effort needed for the implementation along with a plan.

Data Anonymization Implementation Phase: Implements the anonymization solution across the enterprise as per plan.

Operations Phase: Involves ongoing maintenance of the data anonymization solution and ensures adherence to enterprise data privacy policies.

Reference

1. *2010 Annual Study: U.S. Cost of a Data Breach* (Research conducted by Ponemon Institute. LLC and Sponsored by Symantec).

6

Departments Involved in Enterprise Data Anonymization Program

Points to Ponder

- Which are the departments to be involved in a data anonymization program?
- Why should they be involved? Who are the key stakeholders and what are their roles in the program?
- What is the function of the steering committee and who should be part of the steering committee?

Although external consultants should be able to identify the functional and technology requirements for the data anonymization program with minimal help from the organization, we also need to wade through the organizational labyrinth for addressing regulatory compliance requirements. The success of an enterprisewide data anonymization program depends to a large extent on the active participation of various departments.

In this chapter as well, the terms "data privacy" and "privacy" are used interchangeably. Similarly, "data privacy incident," "privacy incident," and "incident" are used interchangeably.

The Role of the Information Security and Risk Department

Most organizations have a centralized department for handling enterprise security and risk. The enterprise security group typically has separate divisions to handle physical security, network security, and information security and data privacy. Organizations serious about data privacy violations also have a chief data officer (CDO) or a chief privacy officer (CPO) heading this division.

The role of the chief privacy officer. (Courtesy of Jophy Joy)

The information security and risk department (some organizations call this the business security department) enables the organization to handle information security and data privacy incidents. This department proactively identifies risks, and implements and maintains enterprisewide information security and privacy policies. They also help audit, monitor, and assist departments in complying with information security and privacy guidelines and policies. Ideally, data privacy-related incidents are also handled by this department and thus the key stakeholder for a data anonymization program would be the information security and risk department. In fact, the trigger for many data anonymization programs is the noncompliance reports raised as part of audits by this department. This department plays a key role in the entire data anonymization program. Table 6.1 details the activities of the representatives of this department.

The Role of the Legal Department

Given that the primary driver of the data anonymization exercise is to ensure that the enterprise complies with various data privacy laws, the involvement of the legal department in this initiative is important. The legal department can enable identification of the data privacy laws or regulations applicable to the enterprise in each region.

Large enterprises, with their presence spread across various countries, need to comply with local privacy regulations. The legal team

Table 6.1   The Role of the Information Risk and Security Group across the End-to-End Data Anonymization Life Cycle

DATA ANONYMIZATION PROGRAM PHASE	ACTIVITIES PERFORMED BY THE INFORMATION SECURITY AND RISK TEAM	DELIVERABLES SOUGHT FROM THE DATA ANONYMIZATION TEAM
Assessment	Provide enterprise data classification policy and guidelines.	Not applicable.
	Sign off on the evaluation criteria for data anonymization tool.	Data anonymization tool evaluation criteria.
Tool evaluation and solution definition	Review evaluation report and provide sign-off for procurement of data anonymization tool. The sign-off should indicate that the tool is appropriate to the organization for anonymization of data from an information privacy perspective and poses no risk to the enterprise.	Evaluation report. Pilot application sample of masked and unmasked records (10–20 records for each technique used in the pilot).
Implementation	Representatives from this department to sign off on the sensitive fields identified for data anonymization. The sign-off should acknowledge that the data anonymization techniques used to anonymize the data fields appropriately protect the privacy of the customer and employee data collected, stored, processed, or transmitted by the application.	The representatives from this department would need to examine 10–20 sample records of unmasked and masked data for each sensitive field.
	Representatives from this department to sign off on the appropriateness of the data anonymization solution. Sign-off on the controls used for protection of data privacy.	Anonymization solution for each application.
Operations	Periodic audit verifying if application data are anonymized before moving out of the production environment for each upgrade/fix. Audit also must confirm that controls are adequate for protection of data privacy for ongoing releases.	Audit inputs.

representatives along with information security and risk group representatives can help in providing guidelines on what type of data need to be marked for privacy compliance for each region. The information security and risk group designs its enforcement and incident response policies and procedures with the active participation of the legal team.

The Role of Application Owners and Business Analysts

Although the legal team helps shortlist the regulations applicable for the enterprise, they would not have a detailed view of the applicable regulations at the level of an IT application. The application owners and business analysts are the ones who would be in the know of the specific regulations relevant to the IT application. (They may in turn consult the legal team for this, however.)

The application owners and the business analysts are the ones who know the data domain handled by the application very well. Thus they play a key role in helping provide confirmation on the sensitivity of the application with respect to data privacy regulations during the assessment phase. During the anonymization implementation phase, they provide the sign-off for sensitive fields identified in the application as well as the anonymization implementation for the application.

The Role of Administrators

Database administrators (DBAs) help in providing access to data stores during anonymization implementation for analysis. They also help provision databases for anonymization. In most organizations, the data flow from production environments to nonproduction environments is managed by DBAs. After anonymization implementation, the DBAs would be the key point of contact for integration of the data anonymization process along with existing data migration processes from production to nonproduction environments.

During the implementation of anonymization, the system administrators help provision the environment needed for implementation of anonymization. They also help in enforcement of security for execution of the data anonymization process.

The Role of the Project Management Office (PMO)

In most medium-to-large enterprises, the PMO comes into the picture for any enterprisewide implementation. The PMO facilitates coordination between multiple departments and teams and helps in managing external consultants, product vendors, and service vendors. Managing the licensing and service contracts with the vendors and partners also falls under the purview of the PMO. In short, the mandate of the PMO would be to complete the data anonymization implementation on schedule within budget with no compromise on quality enterprisewide.

The Role of the Finance Department

Funding for any enterprisewide initiative is always a tougher proposition than a departmentwide initiative due to the shared nature of the investment. Arriving at which department will fund what proportion of the cost is always a tough problem. The outcome of the assessment phase can help provide input for apportioning the cost to each unit. If each individual business unit has its own IT department, the enterprisewide initiative may turn out to be a hard nut to crack.

A typical enterprisewide data anonymization implementation can range from half a million US$ to 5 million US$ based on the scope. The finance department's approval is imperative for kickstarting a program of such a nature. Figure 6.1 shows the extent of involvement of cross-functional units across the enterprise for an end-to-end data anonymization program.

Steering Committee

In most organizations, any initiative spanning multiple departments has a steering committee. The objective of this committee is to meet periodically to take stock of the progress of the initiative, resolve any conflicts of interest, mitigate risks, oversee change management, and steer the program toward a successful end or transition.

Thus if a data anonymization steering committee is to be formed for overseeing end-to-end implementation, it can consist of CPO and Unit Privacy Officers, members from the CFO organization, CIO and CTO organizations, information security and risk department,

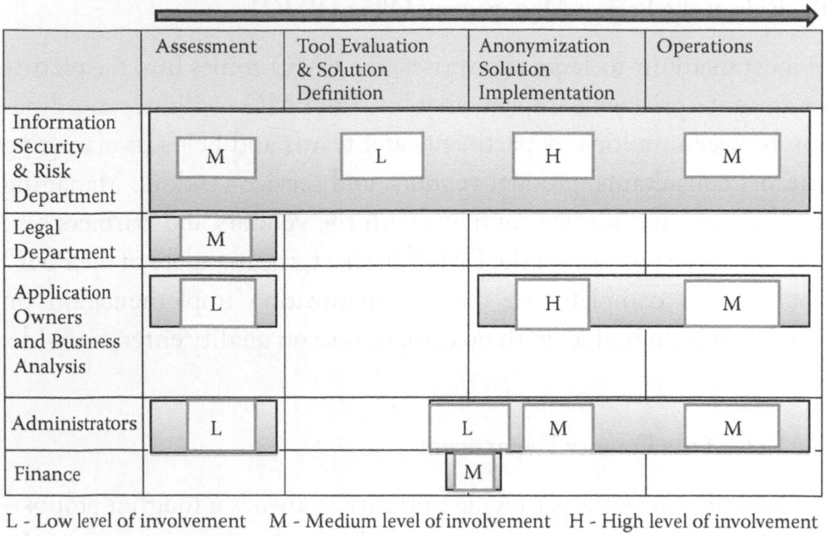

	Assessment	Tool Evaluation & Solution Definition	Anonymization Solution Implementation	Operations
Information Security & Risk Department	M	L	H	M
Legal Department	M			
Application Owners and Business Analysis	L		H	M
Administrators	L		L M	M
Finance			M	

L - Low level of involvement   M - Medium level of involvement   H - High level of involvement

Figure 6.1   Involvement of cross-functional units across the enterprise for an end-to-end data anonymization program.

and legal department apart from the lead program manager of the anonymization programs. The application owners and business analysts can be guest invitees whenever the anonymization of that application comes in for review. Some of the steering committees also include the tool vendor and the service implementation vendor.

Conclusion

For data anonymization programs to succeed, especially enterprise-wide programs, the support of multiple departments is required. In addition to the finance department, which needs to approve the budget for anonymization, and the PMO, which manages the implementation program, the key stakeholders include the following:

Information Security and Risk Department: For providing help on data classification policy, for approval of the data anonymization tool to be procured after reviewing evidence of anonymization, approval of sensitive analysis fields as well as the anonymization solution after going through the evidence of sensitive data being anonymized, for ongoing audits of data privacy anonymization adherence.

Legal Department: For helping identify laws relevant to the enterprise and helping the information security and risk department frame policies against misuse of personal data, as well as enforcement of data privacy protection policies across the enterprise.

Application Owners and Business Analysts: For helping to get through the sensitivity analysis of applications and helping to ensure the anonymization solution integrates with the application processes and does not change the behavior of the application. They also ensure that the data anonymization process is supported for all future application fixes and upgrades.

Administrators: Administrators help in authorization and access to both production data and anonymization environment and help integrate the anonymization scripts with the data migration process from production to nonproduction environments.

7

PRIVACY METER— ASSESSING THE MATURITY OF DATA PRIVACY PROTECTION PRACTICES IN THE ORGANIZATION

Points to Ponder

- Where does the organization stand with respect to maturity in handling personal data of employees, partners, and customers?
- What is the reference model for measuring maturity of data privacy practices in the organization?
- Given the current state of maturity of the organization, what are the activities to be kickstarted before implementing data anonymization?

Assessing the maturity of the data privacy protection practices in the organization gives an indication of where to start the data anonymization program from. The lower the maturity of the organization is, the higher the efforts needed as part of the data anonymization program and the higher the likelihood of an insider data leak and the risk of noncompliance to regulations.

Here is a proposed data privacy protection maturity model, which is also called the "Privacy Meter." This model arrives at the maturity level based on the existing practices followed and attitude toward handling sensitive data of customers and employees.

Level 0:			

State of maturity of data privacy protection practices across the enterprise. (Courtesy of Jophy Joy)

At the lowest level of the data privacy protection model, which is Level 0, there exists an atmosphere of complete trust. Anybody requesting data as part of application development or testing gets easy access and the data also include personal data of employees. The requester is trusted to handle the data for legitimate purposes only. There is no policy classifying data or information and data controls are minimal.

	Level 1		

At this level of maturity, the employees and contractors are aware of the existence of data privacy laws. Whenever a developer or tester requests data, appropriate authorizations are sought, any data that are felt to be "sensitive" by the DBA or application developer are encrypted using SQL scripts, and these data are provided to the requester. The key characteristics at this stage of maturity are:

- Employees and contractors are aware that any misuse of personal data related to customers or employees will affect their organization in a bad way.
- However, there is no help from the organization on what should be considered sensitive and what should not be. The organization

is characterized by a lack of information classification policies. There is a lack of formal guidelines and standards toward preserving customer and employee privacy in the organization.

- Employees try to show their concern by ensuring that personal data are encrypted before sharing using the most practical approach. The flip side of this practical approach is an effort that would have to be made rewriting the SQL encryption scripts whenever there were any technology upgrades or schema changes.
- This state of maturity reflects a state where the employees and contractors are more sensitive than the organizational management toward protection of privacy of the customers.

		Level 2	

This level of maturity reflects a mature approach of the organization toward protection of privacy of customer and employee data. Quite a few large financial organizations have reached this level of maturity. The following are the key characteristics:

- Every department has a mandate to protect sensitive data.
- There is an information security and risk department mandated to create awareness of data privacy rules.
- There exists a formal policy for classifying data into different levels of privacy.
- However, every department can adopt its own way to anonymize data.
- There is no standardized approach toward data privacy preservation and data anonymization. As a result the enterprise ends up with multiple data anonymization tools and tool-specific or ad hoc techniques being used for data anonymization.
- Due to each department using its own approach and technique, an integration test (involving multiple departments) using anonymized data is a big challenge, and many times an integration test is performed with actual data from production without anonymization after getting exception approvals from senior management.

- This is a state where both the employees as well as the management seem to be sensitive toward data privacy protection. However, poor planning and lack of a holistic approach has resulted in suboptimal usage of anonymization and the threat of personal data misuse still looming large.

			Level 3

This is an optimal state of maturity where the enterprise is equipped to prevent any misuse of personal data due to slack internal processes. This level of maturity is characterized by the following:

- A standardized approach toward data privacy preservation is followed and it limits proliferation of anonymization tools across the enterprise.
- Data privacy preservation policies are mature and there is strong enforcement of data privacy preservation policies across the enterprise with regular privacy audits being conducted by the information security and risk group.
- Anonymized data can be used for integration testing and a "dynamic anonymization environment" is supported for application development and testing.
- Privacy modeling is performed as part of the software development life cycle.

Planning a Data Anonymization Implementation

Where the organization stands with respect to the data privacy maturity model provides a good indicator of where to start in the data anonymization cycle.

- If the organization is already at Level 3 maturity then the entire anonymization program can be kickstarted without any pilot and can be implemented quickly.
- If the organization is at Level 2, we may need to find the right anonymization tool among the existing ones or look at the best fit tool externally after an evaluation. Only after the evaluation process can data anonymization implementation begin.

There are many organizations that should be at Level 2 maturity by virtue of having procured a data anonymization tool but end up being at Level 1 maturity as they do not know how to use the tool and end up using SQL scripts for encryption.

- If the organization is at Level 1, then data anonymization implementation can begin only after the organization is ready with information classification policies and strong privacy enforcement policies and procedures. This must be followed by a detailed anonymization tool evaluation and pilot before beginning the implementation of anonymization for sensitive applications across the enterprise.
- If the organization is at Level 0, which is highly unlikely, establishment of an information security and risk group should be the first activity as part of the program.

Table 7.1 summarizes the various levels of maturity of the organization to handle sensitive data.

Conclusion

The data privacy maturity model or the Privacy Meter is a model to understand the as-is state of the enterprise with respect to handling sensitive data. The lower the maturity of the enterprise is, the higher the risk of misuse of sensitive data and the higher the effort and preparatory time needed for data anonymization implementation. As part of the assessment phase, external consultants must provide a view of the current state of the enterprise regarding the Privacy Meter.

Table 7.1   Data Privacy Maturity Model

	LEVEL 0	LEVEL 1	LEVEL 2	LEVEL 3
Organizational attitude to privacy protection	Complete trust	Basic	Standard	Optimized
Employee awareness of need to protect privacy of customer and employee data	Poor	Good	High	High
Information classification policy	Nonexistent	May exist, but employees and contractors unaware of any guidelines for classification of data	Exists	Exists
Organizational readiness for protection of privacy of sensitive data	No readiness	Low	Medium	High
Controls and enforcement	None	None to Low	Low to Medium	High

Coverage of anonymized data for nonproduction environments	None	Low	Medium. Integration test cannot be performed across applications belonging to different departments when necessary with anonymized data.	High. Integration test can be performed across applications belonging to different departments with anonymized data whenever needed.
Probability of misuse of personal data due to insiders	Very high	High	Medium	Low. From a process perspective, no misuse is possible.
Effort for anonymization implementation	Very high	High	Medium	Low
As-is anonymization approach	None	SQL encryption scripts	Tool-based approach. However, different departments may have different anonymization tools and there is no standardization across the enterprise.	Tool-based approach standardized across the enterprise.
Infrastructure	No separate environment for anonymization.	No separate environment for anonymization	Static environment for anonymization	Dynamic environment for anonymization
Process	None	Basic	Ad hoc and Decentralized.	standardized across departments.

8

ENTERPRISE DATA ANONYMIZATION EXECUTION MODEL

Points to Ponder

- What are the different execution models for implementing data anonymization across the enterprise?
- Which model is best suited for the organization?

A typical setup or facility for anonymization implementation comprises:

- Infrastructure for execution of anonymization
- Infrastructure for hosting application data repositories
- Processes for execution of anonymizing sensitive data belonging to the IT applications
- Data anonymization tools
- Supporting tools for data discovery, data cleaning, data subsetting, test data creation
- Prerequisite software for hosting the anonymization tool(s)
- Prerequisite hardware for hosting the anonymization tool(s)

And, of course, it also comprises people for configuring the anonymization tool and executing the anonymization scripts as well as people for managing data services with a governance model around them.

The execution model for the data anonymization model influences the productivity, governance, and costs of the anonymization implementation and operation. The execution model is dependent on the timeframe and the scale planned for the implementation of anonymization throughout the enterprise. If the plan is to cover only a few important applications belonging to one group or department, then a decentralized model should work fine. If the plan is to take up the anonymization of the sensitive applications across the enterprise, then a shared services model or what is being called a factory model makes sense. This chapter describes each of these execution models along with its pros and cons.

Execution models for enterprise data anonymization. (Courtesy of Jophy Joy)

Decentralized Model

In this model, every department or business has its own data anonymization implementation. The anonymization process is well integrated with the application processes and tailored to the specific demands of the department. The best practices are rarely shared across the enterprise. Every department has its own version of an anonymization tool and the enterprise ends up with multiple tools. Figure 8.1 depicts the decentralized execution model.

The typical benefits of this approach are a shorter approval process, shorter implementation time, and highly adaptive processes to suit business needs. On the flip side, there is no standardization or minimal standardization of anonymization tools and processes across the enterprise and there is a higher cost of operations as compared to other execution models.

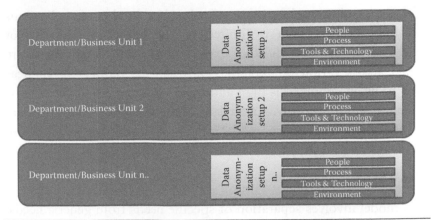

Figure 8.1 Decentralized anonymization setup.

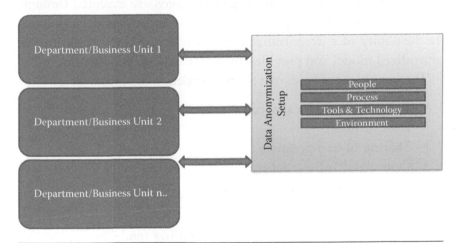

Figure 8.2 Centralized anonymization setup.

Centralized Anonymization Setup

In this model, the entire anonymization setup is centralized. One single unit is responsible for anonymization across the enterprise and every department or business unit must work through this unit. Figure 8.2 depicts the operating model of a centralized anonymization setup.

The benefits to the enterprise include cost savings, easier adoption of best practices, a standardized approach, and higher productivity. The cons of this approach include a longer approval cycle, longer time for decision taking, and slower response to specific needs of the department.

This execution model works well when the number of applications handling sensitive data is limited or the entire program is not time-bound, but falls short of expectations when departments are spread across various geographies or when the number of applications to be anonymized is high and their implementation needs to be managed simultaneously. As a result, more and more enterprises are looking at a shared services model for anonymization implementation.

Shared Services Model

This model involves separation of specific needs from generic needs. All the specific needs of a department are executed as part of the individual department itself and all generic needs are executed through the shared services setup. Thus a shared services model combines the flexibility of a decentralized model with the cost savings of the centralized model and provides an optimized execution model.

The key characteristics of a shared services model include:

- Adaptability to local needs
- Cost savings
- Sharing of best practices
- Optimized Infrastructure
- Ability to handle scale of operations
- Continuous improvement

Many vendors also promise a flexible staffing model as part of the shared services setup. The diagram in Figure 8.3 provides an overview of the operating model of a shared services setup.

The anonymization setup of each department controls the anonymization implementation and operations. Although any specific needs of the department are handled by the department's own setup, the shared services setup provides the generic anonymization needs of the department as a service. Any interaction of the department with the shared services is through the department's own anonymization setup.

One of the key issues to ponder is the location of the shared services anonymization facility. If the shared services facility exists outside the country, movement of data or even access to production data from the facility is going to hit regulatory hurdles. In such a scenario, there is a need to explore shared services for each country.

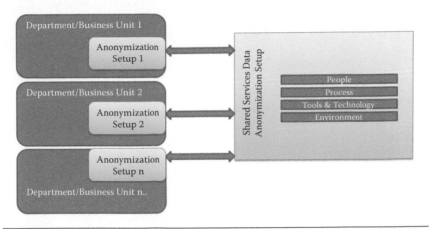

Figure 8.3 Shared services anonymization setup.

Conclusion

Based on the needs of the organization, a decentralized, centralized, or shared services model can be adopted as the execution model for the anonymization implementation. Although a decentralized model is generally the outcome of an unplanned approach toward data anonymization resulting in the proliferation of data anonymization tools and absence of sharing of best practices across the enterprise, a centralized model may end up as a bureaucratic approach, inflexible toward the specific needs of the departments, although it provides cost benefits. Hence many large enterprises are evaluating migration toward a shared services model for benefits of scale and optimizing costs while having the flexibility to attend to specific business or department needs.

9

TOOLS AND TECHNOLOGY

Points to Ponder

- Can data anonymization be implemented without a tool?
- What are the benefits of an anonymization tool for an enterprise data anonymization initiative?
- What is the process for selection of an enterprise data anonymization tool?
- What are the capabilities required for an enterprise anonymization tool?

Data masking can be accomplished easily by just a set of SQL scripts if all the following conditions are true:

- The application stores sensitive data within itself.
- The application does not exchange sensitive data with other applications.
- The application does not receive sensitive data from other upstream applications.
- The sensitive data does not have cross-referential integrity with other applications or other data repositories.
- The number of sensitive fields is few.

However, a self-contained and isolated sensitive data scenario rarely exists. Most applications exchange sensitive data with one or more applications or contain sensitive fields across data repositories.

Many organizations start off using custom-developed SQL scripts for anonymizing sensitive data. These scripts typically use random encryption techniques for masking data in columns. However, the utility of this approach is limited. If data sources belonging to different technologies have to be masked using this approach, the "referential integrity" across data sources cannot be maintained and the integration test is the first casualty. Those embarking on the SQL scripts route for anonymization implementation have fallen into a situation wherein they end up spending an enormous amount of effort on script maintenance whenever there is a change in schema.

Which tool is to be chosen for anonymization? (Courtesy of Jophy Joy)

A tool-based approach to data anonymization can help address the above challenges and provide the following business benefits to the enterprise:

- *Enables data sharing with other teams without the risk of misuse of sensitive information*: De-identified data can be shared across the organization for statistical and other holistic analyses.
- *Enables the enterprise to follow best practices when application development and testing activities are outsourced*: A copy of the production data, which are de-identified, can be safely shared with the application testing and development teams (although they may not be employees of the organization).
- *Cost Savings when calculated over a longer period*: A data masking solution for the enterprise leveraging a data anonymization tool, which is easily customizable, configurable, and supports various platforms, leads to significant cost savings through productivity gains when compared to an SQL-encryption script-based approach.

Thus, investing in a data masking tool, especially when embarking on an enterprisewide anonymization initiative, is a must. An anonymization tool for an enterprise data anonymization can be selected after a two-stage process, namely:

- Shortlisting of tools for evaluation
- Evaluation and selection of the best-fit tool

Shortlisting Tools for Evaluation

The objective of this stage is to shortlist two or three tools for evaluation. The data anonymization tool market can be broadly classified into three categories:

- Pure-play data anonymization tools
- Data anonymization tools that come as part of a test data management suite (data subsetting, test data creation in addition to data anonymization)
- Data anonymization tools that form part of a data management suite of tools (which includes data discovery, database auditing, data subsetting, test data creation, and data archiving in addition to data anonymization)

The shortlist can be arrived at based on answers to the following questions:

- What is the purpose of the data anonymization initiative? Is it for protecting data privacy in nonproduction environments or even for business process operations and technical support in production environments?
- Is the data anonymization part of test data management? What tools are already available in the enterprise for test data management?
- Is the data anonymization part of a larger data management and data security initiative? What tools are already available in the enterprise for data management/data security?
- Is the data anonymization exercise being conducted as part of a larger regulatory compliance initiative such as PCI-DSS compliance or HIPAA compliance?
- Should we pay for a software suite when all we need is one module of the suite?
- What is the best fit for the larger enterprise initiative (be it data security/regulatory compliance/data management/test data management)? Can any of the other nondata anonymization

features that come in as part of the test data management suite, data management suite, and so on, be reused for the other parts of the larger initiative?

Tool Evaluation and Selection

The objective of this phase is to select the right tool for the enterprise data anonymization based on detailed evaluation criteria encompassing functional needs, technology and platform needs, and operational needs in addition to cost and vendor relationship. A typical set of capabilities required to be supported by the enterprise anonymization tool is shown in Figure 9.1.

Functional Capabilities*

This section provides a list of the functional capabilities expected from the tool to be used for an enterprise data anonymization initiative.

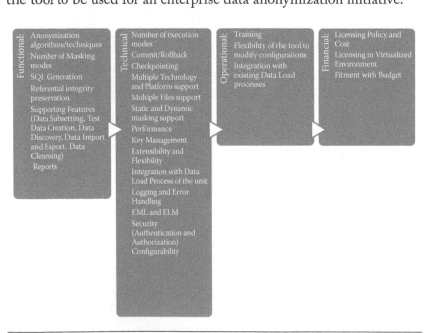

Figure 9.1   Tool evaluation criteria.

---

* Ability to preserve data format and type are treated as basic capabilities required to qualify as a data anonymization tool. Hence they are not treated as an evaluation parameter.

Algorithms/Techniques Supported
- How many algorithms are supported?
- What are the algorithms supported?
- What is the cryptographic strength of the algorithms?
- Are specific algorithms for anonymizing national identification numbers such as SSNs, or national insurance numbers supported?
- Are specific algorithms for generating or formatting SSNs, credit card numbers, addresses, zip codes, or date of birth supported?
- Does the tool support deterministic techniques for anonymization?
- Does the tool support randomized techniques for anonymization?
- Does the tool support unmasking or reverse masking techniques?
- Does the tool support realistic data generation techniques?
- Does the tool allow you to build custom rules?
  - For example, if *firstname* and *lastname* fields are masked, does it support building a rule wherein the *fullname* column/field can be masked with the concatenated values of, say *firstname* and *lastname?*
  - Similarly, for HR systems, the income tax may be based on different slabs. For example, below 30,000 USD p.a. (per annum) there may no income tax, whereas for between 30,000 USD and 50,000 p.a. the tax may be 10% after a standard deduction of say 30,000 USD, for >50,000 USD, the tax may be 30% after a standard deduction of 30,000 USD. In order to support realistic data generation for HR system testing, the anonymization tool must support creation of rules or a formula that is dependent on a standard value or another column.

Number of Masking Modes Supported
- Does it support partial masking?
  - For example, we may need to mask only the last four digits of a credit card number.

- Does the tool support incremental masking?
  - If we get a fresh dump of production data and we already have anonymized data up to last week, does the tool provide a facility to have only anonymized data from last week until today instead of the entire data dump?
  - In the case where we need only the production data from the last few days for, say testing, does the tool make it possible to have only the delta records available for masking before moving this delta dataset to the testing environment? This is especially needed where we already have the masked data available for previous days and a lot of transaction records get generated daily.

Custom SQL Query
- Does the tool provide support for generating/writing custom SQL queries?
- Does the tool support AND/OR queries as well as a combination of multiple masking techniques?
- Does the tool provide support for writing pre- and postprocessing rules?

Referential Integrity Preservation
- Does the tool preserve referential integrity across tables in the same database?
- What is the approach it supports for maintaining referential integrity across data stores? For example, if I mask the customer name in the input file feed and I also have the same customer name in the database, what is the approach recommended by the tool to ensure the same masked value?

Auxiliary Features
 Data Subsetting
- Does the tool support taking only a small data set from the master copy before masking the data?

Test Data Creation
- Do you need to support masking as part of a larger test data management initiative? If yes, does the tool support creation of test data with all the relationship preserved for the test case?

Data Discovery
- Does the tool allow discovery of sensitive data across the enterprise?
- Does the tool allow discovery of relationships from schema?
- Does the tool allow discovery of relationships between data columns?
- Many enterprises run on legacy systems and there is no inventory of the files used by the application. Does the tool provide the capability to identify the files used by the application or program? This problem is widespread in enterprises using mainframe systems.
- Can the tool discover the structure of a file? Can the tool provide the structure of the tool from a COBOL program or a copybook?
- Does the tool scan across ports to provide an inventory of where data reside?

Data Import and Export
- Does the tool allow import and export of sensitive field names? This is especially helpful from a multiuser or enterprisewide perspective.
- Can the sensitive domain/field list (identified as part of another unit's data anonymization implementation) be imported into the tool? Can the sensitive domains identified in the first application that is anonymized be exported onto the enterprise-sensitive domain/field list?
- Does the tool provide an export of selected masked records in an Excel sheet for a limited number of records?

Data Cleansing
- The original data set may have some bad data that need cleaning. Does the tool support cleaning of bad data?

Reports Supported
- Does the tool provide reports about the operational details of anonymization in terms of who masked what field when and using what technique?
- Does the tool report the list of fields masked per application per data store?

- Does the tool support online reporting as well as PDF reports?
- Does the tool support batch mode of PDF report generation and notification of the report as an email attachment?

Technical Capabilities

This section provides a list of the technical capabilities expected from the tool to be used for an enterprise data anonymization initiative.

Number of Execution Modes Supported: (Online/Batch)
- Does the tool support scheduling of masking jobs?
- For a small dataset, if we need to mask immediately, does the tool support online masking?

Commit/Rollback
- It is possible that due to bad data, masking may error out after masking a part of the original (unmasked) data set. Does the tool support rollback of the masked data set?

Checkpointing
- Will the tool be able to restart masking from the record where it failed?

Multiple Technology and Platform Support   Given the spread of different versions of heterogeneous technology across the enterprise, this is an important requirement.

- Does the tool support the last few versions of the data store technology?
- Is the tool compatible with different operating systems such as Linux, UNIX, or Windows?
- Does it support all technologies where you store confidential data (database, files, message queue)?
- What types of databases are supported for masking?
  - Mainframe (DB2, IMS, IDMS)?
  - Oracle, SQL Server, Sybase, PostGRESQL, MySQL?
  - What versions of databases are supported? Does it support the versions used in the enterprise?

Support for Multiple File Formats
- Does the tool support masking of xml, txt?
- Does the tool support industry format files (SWIFT, EDI, etc.)?
- Does the tool support masking of fixed length files?
- Does the tool support masking of delimited files?
- Does the tool support masking of VSAM and QSAM files?

Support for Both Static and Dynamic Masking
- Does the tool support masking of data in motion apart from data at rest?

Performance
- What is the volume of data supported for masking? If there is a need for a fresh dump of data from production for testing an application, the anonymization of these data shouldn't take days for completion. Although subsetting can be used for most scenarios, there are scenarios where the entire anonymized data set from production may be needed, for example, performance testing.

Key Management
- Anonymization for integration test of applications leverage symmetric encryption algorithmic techniques. For data coming in from upstream systems, symmetric encryption algorithms are used for masking and when data move from application to downstream systems, decryption algorithms are used for unmasking. The keys used for encryption need to be managed in a secure fashion in order to protect them from misuse. They need to be stored securely and generated periodically. Any distribution of keys must also be through a secure channel.

Extensibility and Flexibility
- The architecture of the tool must be modular. Other applications must be able to invoke the anonymization algorithms through an API or a web service, especially for scenarios where we may need to anonymize data from a dynamic masking perspective.

Integration with Data Load Process

- In large organizations when data need to be made available for testing, typically multiple groups are involved. There is a separate group for provisioning data and a different group that may execute the anonymization scripts. The anonymization scripts may need to be automatically executed after the entire data dump is made available. My observation has been that unless the anonymization process can be integrated totally with the data load process of the enterprise/group, the adoption rate of the data anonymization process is pretty low.

Logging and Error Handling

- End users should be able to report any issue through friendly logs. The tool should generate error logs and if necessary, these can be viewed by the tool interface. Users should be able to identify whether the exception or error is due to bad data or whether it is a system error and report the system errors to the tool support personnel.

Extract-Mask-Load or Extract-Load-Mask (on Target Data Store)

- Extract-Mask-Load involves anonymizing the data as and when the tool receives the data.
- Extract-Load-Mask involves getting production data onto a staging database, masking them, and generating the anonymized data store.

Ideally, both the above patterns must be supported by the tool. Both these patterns are detailed in a later chapter.

Security: Authorization and Authentication

- Only authenticated users should be allowed to log on to the tool and use the tool.
- Some enterprises require a further granular level of security where there is authorization required even for execution of masking. Different roles have different levels of access here. A few roles will have access to view the configurations but not preview or execute the algorithms.
- Audit logs should also be generated to identify who executed the masking tool when and on what data store.

- The tool must ensure that connection strings are encrypted in the configuration files.

Configurability

- Any new sensitive fields getting added or deleted as part of application upgrades shouldn't result in building the anonymization configuration from scratch. The tool should provide the ability to add new fields or remove fields for masking incrementally into the configuration files.

Operational Capabilities

This section provides a list of the operational capabilities expected from the tool to be used for an enterprise data anonymization initiative.

- Does the tool vendor provide exhaustive training along with materials for adoption of the tool across the enterprise?
- How flexible is the tool to accommodate new data sources or formats for masking? Will the vendor provide an upgrade to the tool?
- Can the tool be integrated with data load processes so that the masking process can be done overnight or on weekends?

Financial Parameters

This section provides a list of the financial parameters for deciding on the tool to be used for an enterprise data anonymization initiative.

- What is the licensing policy of the tool? Is the license per user or per GPU, CPU cores, CPU, data sources, or on the basis of the number of records masked?
- How does the licensing cost work out in a virtualized environment?
- The tool may provide some features we may not need. Does the tool vendor require us to pay for the entire suite or can we select (and pay for) only the tool capabilities we need on an à la carte basis?

- How does the licensing cost fit into your budget? What is the customization cost of the tool? What is the professional services and consulting cost for implementation of the tool? What are the hardware and infrastructure costs for supporting the tool? What is the total cost of operation of the tool?

DATA ANONYMIZATION TOOLS ON THE MARKET

The data anonymization tool market is crowded with a mix of pure-play data masking tool vendors, test data management vendors, and data management vendors. The popular data anonymization tool vendors on the market include Camouflage, IBM, Oracle, Grid-Tools, Infosys, TCS, Wipro, Axis Technology LLC, Informatica, Ab-Initio, Solix, among others. (This vendor list is not ordered on the degree of their popularity.)

While most of the tools more or less meet the standard anonymization requirements of any enterprise, each seems to have its own areas of strength. The decision to go ahead with any tool more or less boils down to its evaluation on financial parameters as well as the strength of the relationship of the vendor with the enterprise. The one that fits the budget of the enterprise and has good vendor relationship strength as well as meets the enterprise data anonymization requirements gets the highest preference for selection.

CERTIFIED ANONYMIZATION TOOLS

Given that the anonymization tool will be used to protect the privacy of sensitive enterprise data, some of the information risk departments require the product to be certified for security as per international standards such as common criteria evaluation. Their objectives for seeking a certified product are to ensure that:

1. The product does not store original data and ensures that data privacy protection standards are compatible with the various privacy regulations.

2. The anonymization product is safe.
3. The product supports algorithms that can anonymize data and the anonymized value is irreversible.
4. Encryption techniques supported are of high strength.

While there are no second thoughts about certification as per common criteria security evaluation being a proof of the existence of high security standards of the product, certification is an expensive process. Due to the testing of the product in a stringent security environment, there may be a need to disable some of the productivity enhancing features. Also, it may not be practical for the vendors to ensure certification of minor version upgrades. All said and done, vendors have to recover the cost of the expensive certification from their customers and hence the price of a certified product will always be much higher than a noncertified one. We need to decide whether the sense of security assurance provided by certification is worth the cost.

Scoring Criteria for Evaluation

Before the tool evaluation, we will need to look at the must-have features necessary for the enterprise, nice-to-have, not relevant, not necessary features or parameters. Weightage assigned to the must-have feature can be higher and the overall score for each of the tools can be arrived based on the weightages. Anyway, the most important deciding factor would be the financial parameters and the tool whose TCO fits in with our budget.

Conclusion

Most medium to large enterprises use various repositories such as databases, files, and queues to store sensitive data about customers and employees. The databases may belong to heterogeneous technologies including Oracle, Sybase, Microsoft SQL Server, MySQL, or DB2, among others. The files through which these data are transmitted may belong to various formats such as fixed length format (every record contains a defined start position and end position), delimited format (each field in a record is separated using a special character as delimiter), EDI, and XML files. They may also be exchanged across applications and partners through message queues belonging to various technologies such as TIBCO, IBM MQ Series, or Microsoft MSMQ, etc.

When sensitive personal data are spread across such a wide territory, the assessment phase will most likely make a recommendation for doing away with usage of SQL scripts and use a data masking tool along with supporting tools for implementing data anonymization. Given the expensive licensing costs associated with procuring a data masking tool along with supporting tools across the enterprise, it makes sense to evaluate the tool based on defined criteria. These criteria should define the functional, architectural (nonfunctional), technical, and operational capabilities against which the tool would be measured apart from the associated full-blown financial costs.

10

ANONYMIZATION IMPLEMENTATION— ACTIVITIES AND EFFORT

Points to Ponder

- What are the typical activities performed as part of anony-mization implementation?
- What are the parameters based on which we can arrive at a reusable model to estimate the efforts needed for anonymiz-ing all the sensitive applications across the enterprise?

Once the enterprise is aware of what data needs to be considered sensi-tive, where this data resides (which applications and data stores handle sensitive data), who handles sensitive data and have the governance model as well as processes and guidelines to handle sensitive data as well as handle incidents of sensitive data leakage, it can be considered to be ready with the pre-requisites required for implementing data anonymization across the enterprise. At this stage, apart from the right data anonymization tool, the enterprise would be keen to under-stand the effort involved in anonymizing the sensitive applications across the enterprise. This effort would be the sum of the effort for anonymizing each sensitive application.

The predictability of the estimates for an anonymization initiative would be based on the availability or ability to build an estimation model. One of the approaches for arriving at a good estimation model involves decomposing the set of activities into a granular level, having criteria for identifying the complexity of the application, and having a ready-reckoner for identifying the effort needed for each granular activity for each application based on the complexity level.

Guesstimate or estimate? (Courtesy of Jophy Joy)

Anonymization Implementation Activities for an Application

Here is a break-down of the various activities involved as part of the anonymization implementation for an application. The activities have been grouped based on the teams performing these activities.

Application Anonymization Analysis and Design

These activities would typically be performed by the anonymization implementation team. The implementation team identifies the data sources, stores and sinks of the application, and proceeds with a detailed sensitivity analysis of these. Based on an analysis of the existing application architecture, the anonymization solution (anonymization patterns and techniques to be used) is arrived at. The objective is to arrive at the best fit solution for integrating the data anonymization process into the existing application's data management processes considering the environment as well as the non-functional requirements (performance, security, etc.) under which the solution has to function.

Availability of application documentation (especially for legacy applications) is a key deciding factor for estimating the effort spent on these activities.

Anonymization Environment Setup

These activities would typically be performed by the IT/infrastructure team and not the anonymization implementation team. The objective is to create the optimal "anonymization environment" for the application.

Most of the time, the anonymization environment setup is about securing the existing test environment and may not need too much effort if only a static environment is needed. However, when an integration-test environment is required, the effort involves setting up a new environment.

Application Anonymization Configuration and Build

These activities would be performed by the anonymization implementation team. The objective here is to create the anonymized data for the application by implementing the recommended solution using the anonymization tool (or scripts) in the environment setup for anonymization. These activities must ensure the seamless integration of the anonymization solution with the application data flow. The capabilities or the familiarity of the anonymization team with the tool as well as the application technology and the customization needed for the tool also affect the effort estimates.

Anonymized Application Testing

These activities would typically be performed by the application testing team. The anonymization effort for the application is deemed to be ready only after the application testing team validates that the use of anonymized data has not changed the behavior of the application. This is done by the application team testing the application with anonymized data. This would typically need about two or three rounds of testing.

Complexity Criteria

The complexity of the anonymization implementation varies based on the

- Application characteristics and
- Environment dependencies

Application Characteristics

The anonymization implementation effort depends on the following characteristics of the application:

Quantitative Parameters   Quantity matters!! The key considerations would be

- From how many data stores does the application use data?
- How many tables, files, messages (queued), and the like contain sensitive information?

If the data stores maintain referential integrity with each other, the tool must be capable of supporting cross-data-store referential integrity.

The Data Store Technology Used   The tool needs to support anonymization of data in relevant technology. Tool support for legacy technology is a challenge.

Age of the Application   Anonymization of legacy applications typically needs more effort as it is difficult to find the files being handled by the application. Lack of documentation of these applications leads to difficulties in identifying the format/structure of these files.

Standalone versus Integrated Applications   The integration approach between the application in scope and upstream/downstream applications is an important factor in deciding the anonymization approach, i.e., whether static masking or dynamic masking is to be used.

The number of integration interfaces for the system (especially the number of input source applications) as well as the number of upstream and downstream applications impacts the anonymization effort in a big way. This holds good especially when an integration test is to be performed using anonymized data. For such cases, we would need an automated integration test environment.

Availability of Documentation   Lack of application documentation has the potential to impede the progress of anonymization.

Environment Dependencies

The anonymization implementation effort also depends on the following environmental dependencies of the application:

Number of Servers Available for Anonymization Environment   The creation of a separate environment for anonymization needs time. An application's anonymization implementation can be deemed to be complete for operational purposes after testing of the application with anonymized data.

Most service providers and tool vendors will not be able to provision this effort (needed for creation of a separate environment) as part of their estimates for implementation and it is up to the IT department or application owners to provision this environment.

Some of the other considerations include a virtualized environment or procurement of any hardware and software needed for the anonymized environment. The anonymized environment needs to be ready for each application before testing of the application with the anonymized data.

Security Controls   The anonymization environment would generally lie inside the firewall and the security controls for this environment would be similar to that of a high security environment. Effort also needs to be provisioned for testing the tool in the controlled anonymized environment.

Arriving at an Effort Estimation Model

Arriving at an effort estimation model for anonymization implementation would involve the following steps:

- Definition of complexity criteria
- Ready-reckoner preparation
- Determination of the complexity of the application to be anonymized
- Assignment of effort to each activity based on the ready-reckoner

Both the complexity criteria and ready-reckoner need to be defined only once and can be reused for all applications. Based on experience, the ready-reckoner can be fine-tuned for accuracy.

An anonymization implementation takes anywhere from one or two calendar months to more than six calendar months for completion based on the application characteristics and environment dependencies. Rather than a big-bang approach of anonymizing all sensitive applications across the enterprise, it is better to first start with a pilot, understand the challenges, and then plan a phased implementation based on the application priority and sensitivity levels of the application. It would be easiest to start with a standalone application with no upstream or downstream applications having only a standard RDBMS for anonymization.

The estimation should assume that the prerequisites are in place and dependencies will be met. The prerequisites here would be the preparedness and readiness of the organization for anonymization in terms of established governance mechanism, information security and data classification policies, and procurement of the appropriate tool based on detailed evaluation criteria.

Case Study

Let's take a sample case study to arrive at a ball-park estimation model for the anonymization implementation across the enterprise.

Context

Our bank named *OurBanque* has embarked on an enterprisewide data anonymization initiative. The bank has a portfolio of 600 applications. An assessment exercise has confirmed that 100 applications handle sensitive data in one way or another and we need to arrive at the high-level effort estimate for implementing anonymization across the enterprise. We have decided to take a de-risked approach and have planned to pilot tool-based anonymization beginning with application LOANADM.

Application LOANADM is a desktop application dealing with loan administration and based on an earlier assessment exercise, this application has been categorized as a sensitive application storing loanee personal data. It is a standalone application and has no integration with upstream or downstream applications. The only data store from which it accesses data is a PostGRESQL database with 100 tables.

This is the first of the applications that needs to be anonymized as part of the enterprise anonymization initiative and there is no estimation model in place. We need to arrive at how long it would take to implement anonymization for the application and also devise a model for estimating the entire enterprise anonymization initiative.

Estimation Approach

In order to arrive at a ball-park estimation for the implementation effort across the enterprise, let's follow the standard steps, namely:

- Arriving at *repeatable* complexity criteria
- Deriving a *repeatable* ready-reckoner
- Identifying the complexity of the application
- Arriving at the detailed estimate

The repeatable complexity criteria can be arrived at based on the number of sensitive tables, names of input files that are sensitive, and number of output files that are sensitive. These criteria will help in grouping the applications into a very low complexity, low complexity, medium complexity, high complexity, or very high complexity bucket.

Typically a very low complexity application has less number of sensitive tables and no sensitive input files or output files, no upstream applications and no downstream applications with which it exchanges data. As the complexity level increases, the number of tables with sensitive data, number of input and output files with sensitive data, as well as the number of sensitive upstream and downstream applications increase.

A ready-reckoner can be created to depict a map of the effort needed for each of the application anonymization implementation activities against different complexity levels (very low, low, medium, high and very high).

Application Characteristics for LOANADM

- 100 tables
- No upstream or downstream applications
- No input or output files

Let's assume the sensitivity ratio (ratio of sensitive tables to overall tables in the database) based on an average is less than 20%. Thus for this application, the number of sensitive tables is less than 20. Taking into consideration the other parameters, we can safely assume that this is an application of very low complexity.

Arriving at a Ball Park Estimate

For this sample application (LOANADM), based on the ready reckoner, the total effort would be the sum of the application anonymization analysis and design activities effort, application anonymization build and configuration effort, anonymized application testing effort, and anonymization environment support effort for a very low complexity application.

The anonymization environment setup can be accomplished in parallel before the anonymization build and configuration activities and will be performed by mostly the organization's own IT team and the start to end elapsed duration of the project can be adjusted accordingly.

To arrive at the estimate for the entire sensitive application portfolio (100 applications) across the enterprise, we would need to distribute the applications across various complexity levels and then arrive at the total estimate.

ANONYMIZATION ENVIRONMENT SETUP

Typically, most enterprises set up an anonymization environment for a set of applications than for an individual application to optimize the infrastructure requirements (and cost) for anonymization.

Conclusion

One of the approaches for arriving at an estimation model would be:

- To decompose the implementation activities to a granular level
- To define complexity criteria and create a ready-reckoner
- To classify the application (to be anonymized) into a defined complexity bucket based on the criteria
- To estimate the activities as per the ready-reckoner

Anonymization implementation would involve activities including anonymization analysis and design, anonymization environment setup, tool customization, anonymization script configuration, and application testing (with anonymized data) activities. Estimation for these activities needs to be factored into any anonymization implementation.

Estimates vary based on application characteristics such as quantitative aspects of sensitive elements in the application, integration complexity, use of legacy technology, age of the application, and availability of documentation as well as environmental dependencies including provisioning of hardware, software, infrastructure, and virtualization needs and security controls. Complexity levels of the application can be defined based on these characteristics.

Effort can be assigned to each of the anonymization activities based on the application complexity level and can be summed up to understand the overall effort. As a risk mitigation strategy, an enterprise anonymization initiative can begin with an anonymization pilot of representative applications and then a phased implementation based on priority and sensitivity level of applications can be planned out instead of a big-bang approach.

11

THE NEXT WAVE OF DATA PRIVACY CHALLENGES

The adoption of cloud, explosion of unstructured data, mobile devices, and social networking sites are bringing in the next wave of data privacy challenges to the enterprise. Information technology departments are under pressure to implement "bring your own device" strategies in their enterprise and allowing employees to collaborate through "social media" channels.

The privacy challenges include:

- How can privacy of data be protected on cloud?
- How can employees be prevented from sharing sensitive or confidential data through social networking sites such as Facebook, Twitter, and the like?
- How do we prevent mobile devices from capturing pictures of sensitive data and uploading them to social networking sites?
- Should social networking sites be blocked for persons handling sensitive data?
- Should employees and contractors be prevented from bringing in camera-enabled mobile phones or smart phones to office premises?
- With field-force mobility programs being rolled out in the enterprise, how do we ensure protection of sensitive data in the case where mobile devices need to store these data?
- How do we ensure masking of sensitive data in unstructured text (documents, reports)?
- How do we mask images?
- How do we protect biometric information?
- How should data privacy be handled for big data analytics?

Solutions to some of the above issues are already available on the market, especially for unstructured text privacy protection and image masking solutions. However, most enterprises continue to adopt the short-term approach of denying employees and contractors access to social networking sites and camera-enabled mobile devices in their office premises. One of the effective ways to encourage right practices is to train employees in responsible behavior when using social networks and mobile devices. But enforcing these controls are where enterprises are facing challenges given that existing enterprise data privacy policies haven't yet taken a position on use of mobile devices and social media channels.

As a sponsor for enterprise data privacy initiatives, I would like to leave you with these thoughts on the next wave of challenges in the data privacy protection space. Solutions to address these data privacy challenges are the areas that cry for your attention and funding in the immediate future.

The next part takes an implementer's view toward data anonymization.

PART II
DATA ANONYMIZATION PRACTITIONER'S GUIDE

This section of the book is meant for data anonymization practitioners who may be data architects, application architects, systems architects, technology leads, or specialists. This section takes a look at the types of data masking, the different data anonymization patterns and techniques, and the data anonymization implementation activities.

We start off in Chapter 12 with an overview of the data anonymization patterns and their categorization based on data state, anonymization environment, and data flow.

We then continue with the details of the different patterns available for anonymization of data based on their data state in Chapter 13. Here we take a closer look at static masking and dynamic masking.

After discussion on the different patterns available for anonymizing data based on their data state, we examine in Chapter 14 the different patterns applicable for anonymizing data needed to test applications in a standalone environment as well as an integration test environment.

We then move on in Chapter 15 to discussion of the patterns for integrating anonymization solutions with the existing flow of data from production to nonproduction environments.

After the discussions on different anonymization patterns, it is time to understand the different techniques for anonymizing data. In Chapter 16, we take a look at the different techniques for anonymization of data and the situations where these can be used.

Armed with the understanding of different anonymization patterns and techniques, we move on to Chapter 17 where we can understand how to implement data anonymization for an application and the different activities involved in a data anonymization implementation.

12

DATA ANONYMIZATION PATTERNS

Points to Ponder

- Which are the data anonymization pattern categories?
- Which are the data anonymization patterns?
- How is a pattern and pattern category relevant to the data anonymization solution?

Pattern Overview

In case you, as a data anonymization practitioner, have directly jumped onto this chapter before reading the other chapters in this book, data masking or data anonymization or data scrubbing or data obfuscation or data de-identification are some of the key approaches for preventing misuse of sensitive data.

There are various patterns for implementing data masking. These patterns can be categorized into data state patterns, patterns to anonymize different types of nonproduction environments, and patterns to anonymize flow of sensitive data between different environments. Figure 12.1 depicts the hierarchy of anonymization implementation patterns.

A complete data anonymization solution would typically be a composite mix of pattern categories.

ANONYMIZATION PATTERN OVERVIEW.

Which pattern should I choose? (Courtesy of Jophy Joy)

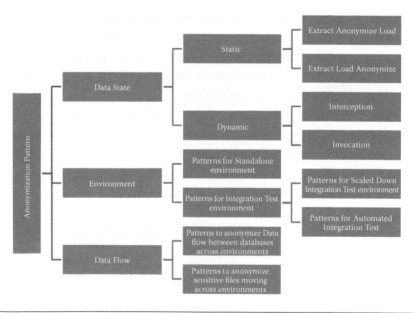

Figure 12.1 Data anonymization pattern hierarchy.

Conclusion

An anonymization solution would need to address the following:

- State of sensitive data
  - Are the data at rest or in motion?
  - Are the sensitive data being received, stored, or transmitted?
- Environment
  - What is the target usage of anonymized data?
  - Where are the anonymized data going to be used?
  - Are the anonymized data going to be needed for an integration test?
- Data Flow
  - Where are the sensitive data going to come from before anonymization?
  - Where will they go to after anonymization?

Thus, an anonymization solution would comprise one of the patterns being chosen from each pattern category.

13

DATA STATE ANONYMIZATION PATTERNS

Points to Ponder

- How can you provide application developers and testers with realistic production data (referential integrity between data entities being preserved) while preventing them from using PII and PHI?
- How can you prevent privileged users of the system such as database administrators (DBAs) from using PII or PHI?
- How can you prevent users of the system including business processing staff and technical support staff from accessing PII or PHI?

Anonymization applied to data at rest, especially from a nonproduction perspective, is called static masking, whereas anonymization applied to data in motion is called dynamic masking.

Principles of Anonymization

The key anonymization principles can be divided into mandatory and optional principles. The mandatory anonymization principles are:

- Referential integrity of the dataset must be preserved after anonymization.
- Data type of the anonymized data must be the same as the input data.

The optional anonymization principles are:

- Anonymized data need to be realistic (when there is no need for encryption).
- Length of anonymized data must match the length of the input (de-anonymized) data.

DATA STATE PATTERNS

Are sensitive data being received, stored, or transmitted by the application?
(Courtesy of Jophy Joy)

- Format of the anonymized data must match that of the input (de-anonymized) data.

Static Masking Patterns

Static masking or the anonymization of data at rest typically includes anonymization of data in databases or static files using different anonymization techniques. See Figure 13.1. Application developers and testers like to use production data for their applications because this increases the probability of detecting issues that can potentially occur in production. The static masking pattern fits in directly with requirements where the production database of the application has to be made available to development and test environments after anonymizing sensitive data.

The patterns used for generating anonymized data using static masking include the EAL (extract-anonymize-load) pattern and

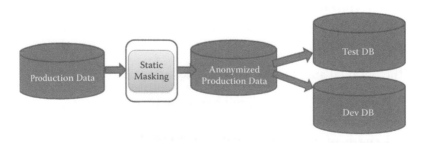

Figure 13.1   Static masking use cases.

the ELA (extract-load-anonymize) pattern. Static masking is used mostly for anonymizing data for nonproduction use cases such as application development and testing.

EAL Pattern (Extract–Anonymize–Load Pattern)

This pattern is used when data in production databases are required for application development or for testing. Data are *extracted* from production, *anonymized,* and *loaded* into the target database (nonproduction database). This is typically done as a batch operation. Most often, only the incremental data are anonymized. Figure 13.2 depicts the EAL pattern.

There are operational challenges in leveraging this pattern as many enterprises do not allow any application to connect to the production database, unless mandatory for production operations as part of their security policies. Many enterprises adopt a variation of the EAL pattern for creating an anonymized replica for nonproduction uses. Here, a file extract is created from the production database. This file is then anonymized and loaded onto the nonproduction database as shown in Figure 13.3.

ELA Pattern (Extract–Load–Anonymize Pattern)

Most organizations don't allow connection of external tools directly to the production database. Instead, a copy of a production database

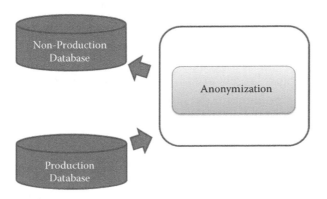

Figure 13.2   Anonymization performed using the extract-anonymize-load (EAL) pattern.

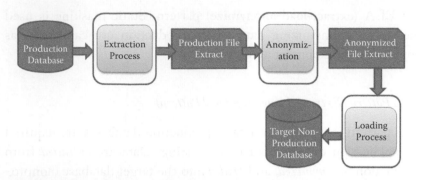

Figure 13.3   Variation of the extract-anonymize-load (EAL) pattern.

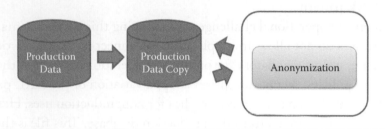

Figure 13.4   Anonymization performed using the extract-load-anonymize (ELA) pattern.

is provided for nonproduction purposes such as application development or maintenance and testing activities. See Figure 13.4.

Anonymization of sensitive data being performed on a copy of the production database is an example of an ELA pattern. This is an easier approach for anonymization operationally, but care needs to be taken to ensure that the copy of the production database is not available for nonproduction usage inadvertently without anonymization.

Data Subsetting

Data subsetting is largely used in association with static masking. As the data in the production database keep growing, it becomes expensive to provision similar infrastructure for the various testing environments and hence test environments generally have a scaled-down infrastructure (especially from a storage perspective).

In order to ensure that the quality of testing does not suffer due to scaled-down infrastructure, data subsetting is increasingly being adopted. Data subsetting (Figure 13.5) is the process of creating

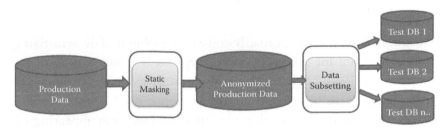

Figure 13.5 Data subsetting.

a subset of production data (anonymized) relevant to the test cases being executed. The subset can be created either based on subsetting criteria, which can be date range or any other dimension or rule, but the key requirement is that referential integrity must still be preserved. For example, if we need to test the latest upgrade to a customer transaction system, the data subset should contain not only the customer records (anonymized) for the specified date range, but also the related customer transaction records.

Benefits Data subsetting provides substantial cost savings, especially the cost of data storage. Let's assume the following about the customer transaction system whose upgrade needs to be tested:

- The production database has grown to 1 TB.
- The enterprise software development life cycle policy mandates that any application upgrade needs to be tested in four different environments (namely the functional test environment, integrated test environment, performance test environment, and acceptance test environment) and signed off before being moved to production.

If data subsetting is not used, then the storage needs for testing would be 1 TB for each environment, i.e., a total of 4 TB of storage.

If data subsetting is adopted, then the total storage required is drastically reduced. The storage needs would be 1 TB for the master anonymized copy (also called the gold copy) and a few gigabytes of data for each environment (based on the subsetting criteria). This would be substantially less than the 4 TB of data requirement.

Dynamic Masking

Although static masking broadly solves the problem of de-sensitizing production data for nonproduction purposes, it is not a good fit for preventing misuse of data in a production environment. Role-based authorization can be used if an application is used as the interface to the user and the application prevents the data from appearing on the screens based on the user's role. But again this does not work for scenarios such as preventing misuse of data by DBAs or technical support personnel who may directly connect to the database.

Wherever the required solution is to ensure that the data in the underlying data store are unchanged, but the data are changed or de-sensitized when the user views them, dynamic masking is the right fit. Dynamic masking is the anonymization of data in motion.

In Figure 13.6, the use of dynamic masking for the fname or first name fields ensures that the user sees the fname or first name of the customer as "Jim" when it is actually "Don."

Dynamic Masking Patterns

Dynamic masking can be achieved through:

- An invasive approach (which requires a code change)
- A noninvasive approach (which is more of a configuration change).

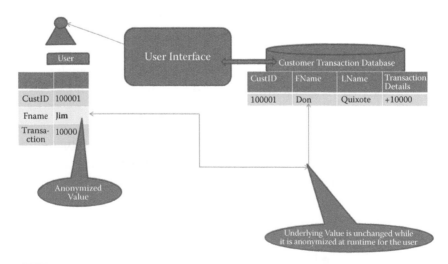

Figure 13.6   Dynamic masking in action.

LAYERED ARCHITECTURE

Legacy applications were mostly built without any separation of responsibilities. Any small change in a function would end up affecting the application in an unexpected area. This made maintenance of the code very difficult.

Layered architecture is a software architecture pattern where the application is logically decomposed into a set of layers to ensure separation of responsibilities. Thus the presentation layer code is responsible for presenting the user interface, the service layer is responsible for exposing the functionality of the application as services, the business layer is responsible for processing the business logic, and the data access layer (DAL) is responsible for access to the data store (database). In a layered architecture, the topmost layer can call only the layer below it and not above it. Thus the business layer can call the DAL, but cannot invoke the layers above it such as the service layer or presentation layer.

An interception pattern is an example of a noninvasive approach and an invocation (pattern) of an anonymization library is a case of an invasive approach. Dynamic masking is increasingly being used for the following scenarios:

- Business process outsourcing
- Technical support outsourcing
- Preventing privileged users such as DBAs from viewing sensitive data

Interception Pattern

In the sample layered architecture shown in Figure 13.7, the presentation layer can either be a web-based application or a desktop application.

In this interception pattern, data are anonymized by either intercepting the data at the presentation layer, the data layer, or even at the service layer. The use of a masking interceptor requires a technology or protocol that allows proxies to be generated.

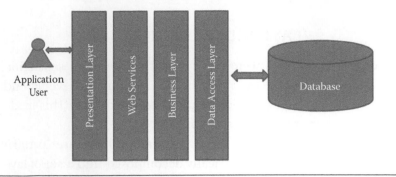

Figure 13.7 Sample application architecture.

While the HTTP-based (Web User Interface or Web Service) interceptions need no code changes in the application, there would be a need to reconfigure the application to enable the request and response to pass through the masking interceptor. Also the masking interceptor may have to be customized extensively.

Data layer interception would leverage a masking interceptor, which is more like a database proxy through which any database query has to pass through. The query coming in is transformed by the data layer interceptor as per the configured rules, and the sensitive fields returned as part of query results are anonymized. This approach does not need any code change in the application and can be applied to business process outsourcing, production support scenarios, or privileged user anonymization scenarios as well as for data movement from production to nonproduction environments. While the data layer interceptors need no code changes in the application and are mostly out-of-the box implementations, they may not be able to support multiple database technologies and data sources like files and messages in queues. This pattern is slowly gaining adoption among large enterprises, and there are commercial tools available in the market.

The approach for intercepting data thus varies based on architecture as well as technology as shown below.

When Should Interception Patterns be Selected and on What Basis?

Table 13.1 aids in selection of the appropriate dynamic masking pattern based on the application architecture.

Table 13.1   Application Architecture—Dynamic Masking Pattern Mapping

ARCHITECTURAL LAYERS	DYNAMIC MASKING PATTERN	SELECTION CRITERIA
1-Web-based user interface as presentation layer, 2-Web service, 3-Business layer, 4-Data access layer, 5-Database	HTTP (presentation layer) interception or Web service interception or Data layer interception.	Pattern selected based on ease of effort and technology support.
1-Web-based user interface as presentation layer, 2-Business layer, 3-Data access layer, 4-Database	HTTP (presentation layer) interception or Data layer interception.	Pattern selected based on ease of effort and technology support.
1-Web-based user interface as presentation layer, 2-Business layer, data access and 3-Data layer are combined	HTTP (presentation layer) interception or Data layer interception based on ease of effort and technology support.	Pattern selected based on ease of effort and technology support.
Web-based application, but layered architecture is not implemented. The presentation layer, business layer, data layer, and data access layer functionalities are all combined.	Data layer interception or HTTP interception	Pattern selected based on ease of effort and technology support.
Client server application (without layers)	Data layer interception	Pattern selected based on technology support.
Client server application with 1-presentation layer, 2-service layer, 3-business layer and data access layer	Web service interception or data layer interception	Pattern selected based on ease of effort and technology support.

In the table, some of the entries in the *Architectural Layers* column have been numbered for a specific purpose. The least number, i.e., 1, denotes the nearest or topmost layer to the user, and the highest number denotes the bottommost layer.

If the architectural layer entries are "1-Web-based User Interface as Presentation Layer, 2-Web Service, 3-Business Layer, 4-Data Access Layer and 5-Database," the request data moves from presentation layer to Web service to business layer to data access layer to database when the user performs an action on the application and the response moves in the opposite direction.

Challenges Faced When Implementing Dynamic
Masking Leveraging Interception Patterns

Despite there being no code changes to existing applications using the interception pattern, there are complex challenges to the implementation of data anonymization when leveraging these patterns such as:

1. *Handling user updates and compressed data transmission*: The masking interceptor should be able to determine when the user has made an update to sensitive fields and have an approach to handle this. It should also be able to handle scenarios where data are exchanged between layers in a compressed format and ensure that the interception process does not have a major impact on performance.
2. *Industrial strength out-of-the box dynamic masking solutions in the market*: Other than the tools available in the market for data layer interception (which may not support all database technologies in an enterprise), most of the other tools are not out-of-the box implementations. They are custom solutions which would be built over a basic set of components based on the requirement.
3. *Estimation of effort for dynamic masking implementation*: Effort for dynamic masking implementation varies based on the pattern used as well as the layer where the pattern is applied. The estimation models need to accommodate for these variations.
4. *Ongoing maintenance challenges*: Given the custom nature of the nondata layer masking interceptor, changes to application may result in need for regeneration and potentially additional customization effort for masking proxy interceptors.

Invocation Pattern

If a new application is being developed, an invocation pattern can be used.

Irrespective of whether the application follows a layered architecture or not, the application code needs to be changed to invoke the anonymization libraries through their Application Programming Interfaces (API).

Due to the invasive approach, this is not a popular approach where an existing application (with a large number of screens) containing

ADOPTION OF INVOCATION DYNAMIC MASKING PATTERN

Given that the objective of application testing is to certify that the application version going into the production environment works as expected under a given condition, most enterprise policies mandate that

- The application binary files of the production environment and test environment must be the same and must originate from the same codebase.
- The application must be purged of any piece of code that is relevant for, say test environments, but not for production environments.

The above principles rule out the usage of a dynamic masking invocation pattern if anonymization is needed only for testing purposes. This is because the application code needs to be changed to invoke the anonymization libraries in the test environment and this code change is not a valid requirement for the production environment.

sensitive fields needs to be anonymized. However, this approach may be used where a few new screens or modules are being developed for the application or a new application is being built from scratch.

Application of Dynamic Masking Patterns

Dynamic masking patterns open up possibilities of protecting privacy for scenarios which were previously out of bounds for anonymization. These patterns enable anonymization to be applied at run time based on various contextual parameters like location, role, environment type (shared environment), and device.

Dynamic Masking versus Static Masking

Table 13.2 summarizes the differences between dynamic and static masking.

Table 13.2   High-Level Comparison of Static and Dynamic Masking

	STATIC MASKING	DYNAMIC MASKING
Definition	Anonymization of data at rest (such as in databases and static files)	Anonymization of data in motion or at runtime
When to use	When underlying sensitive data (sensitive data in data source) can be changed	When underlying sensitive data (sensitive data in data source) should not be changed (anonymized)
Relevancy	Nonproduction environments such as application development and testing	Production environments such as business process outsourcing, production support, remote location access
Patterns	EAL, ELA	Interceptor pattern, invocation pattern
Auxiliary or derivative patterns		Location-based dynamic masking, role-based dynamic masking, shared environment dynamic masking
Pros	• Less effort for implementation • Mature tools on the market with out-of-the-box features	• Enables privacy protection for complex scenarios in production environment • Enables location-flexibility for organizations in terms of hosting their operational centers
Cons	• Not suitable for production environments	• Higher effort for implementation • Tools on the market have limited functionality support or are not of industrial strength • High amount of customization needed
Use cases	Test data management	Remote access, mobility applications for banking (field agent automation)

Conclusion

Based on whether the sensitive data are at rest or in motion, static masking and dynamic masking patterns are chosen. Static masking is masking of data at rest. EAL and ELA form the static masking patterns whereas data subsetting is an auxiliary static masking pattern. Static masking patterns are mostly used in nonproduction environments for application testing and development activities. Dynamic masking, which is the anonymization of data in motion, is largely used for protecting data privacy in production environment scenarios. BPO, production support, and DBA access are examples where dynamic masking is relevant.

Dynamic masking patterns are of two types, namely:

1. *Interception pattern*: This pattern helps in anonymization of data without any change to the application code and can be applied at the presentation layer, service layer, or the data access layer.
2. *Invocation pattern*: This pattern relies on an application code change to mask sensitive data and can be applied at any application layer or even to an application which does not have a layered architecture.

Dynamic masking is relevant in protecting privacy in complex scenarios including protecting privacy on mobile devices, location-based masking, role-based masking, and shared environment masking.

14

ANONYMIZATION ENVIRONMENT PATTERNS

Points to Ponder

- Which are the different environments needed as part of the application's entire life cycle? Which environments among these need anonymized data?
- How can the anonymization patterns be applied to each of these environments (for which anonymized data are needed)?

For an application with a database as the source of data, implementing a simple static masking solution is good enough for de-identifying sensitive data. However, in most enterprises, the applications are a lot more complex with files, message queues, and applications also being the source of personal data.

Application Environments in an Enterprise

In a typical enterprise, different environments are created in order to provide varying levels of isolation for an application across its software development life cycle (SDLC) with each environment:

- Requiring different volumes of data
- Having varying data anonymization requirements
- Fulfilling the needs of different stakeholders.

The diagram in Figure 14.1 showcases a map of the SDLC–application environment–stakeholder–data requirement.

All the above environments may or may not be virtualized. Owing to cost and overhead, some of these environments may be cobbled together. In addition to the above shown environments, typically, there is also a training environment that is meant for training the business users of the application. This environment also needs anonymized data.

137

Which anonymization pattern is relevant for this environment? (Courtesy of Jophy Joy)

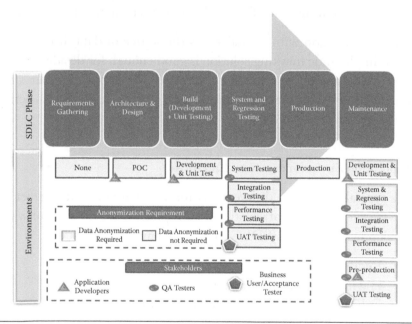

Figure 14.1   SDLC–environment–stakeholder–data requirement mapping.

From Figure 14.1, it is clear that

- Prior to the application going live (in a production environment), anonymized data don't make sense.
- Once the application goes live in production (i.e., in the maintenance phase), any application containing sensitive data

WHAT IS THE INFERENCE FROM THE ABOVE DIAGRAM?

- There is no environment required during the requirements gathering phase.
- There is a need for an environment for conducting POCs (proof-of-concepts) during the architecture and design phase and this environment is used by the application development team. There is no need to anonymize data.
- Similarly, during the build phase, the application developers need an environment for development and unit testing without any data anonymization requirement.
- During the testing phase, various environments such as the functional testing environment, integration testing environment, performance testing environment, and user acceptance testing (UAT) environment have no data anonymization requirement.
- Once the application goes live on production, the maintenance phase needs a variety of environments that need anonymized data. These environments include a development and unit testing environment for application developers, a system and regression testing environment, integration testing environment, and performance testing environment for application testers, and the UAT environment for business users. The preproduction environment will be needed both by application developers and testers.

will need anonymization in all nonproduction environments to ensure protection of data privacy.

Testing Environments

Applications can be tested in either a standalone or an integration environment. Although a standalone environment is good enough for testing the functionality of an application, it does not help validate the application's behavior as per requirements in a complex production environment where the application can receive data from multiple sources, formats, and types of data including upstream and downstream applications. For finding out any potential issues an application may encounter in such environments, an integration test environment is needed. The forthcoming sections detail the patterns used for different types of data sources in different types of environments.

Standalone Environment

This is an environment where the "application to be tested" exists independently with its own set of data sources and sinks. The application is not integrated with any upstream or downstream application. Static masking patterns (EAL and ELA) are the most commonly used patterns in a standalone environment. These have already been discussed in detail in Chapter 13 and in this chapter we focus on the other patterns relevant to a standalone environment.

File Masking Patterns Input files containing sensitive data for an application may be of different formats including fixed length files, variable length with fields separated by a delimiter, XML files, EDI or domain-specific files such as SWIFT files, and the like. Before these files are used for testing, they would have to be desensitized. A standalone environment for an application with input files as the data source is shown in Figure 14.2.

Testing of this application, especially for any fixes, would require a production sample that would need to be anonymized. Anonymized files can be made available for a standalone environment as shown in Figure 14.3.

Typically the source folder may be the location where files are archived or these can be copies from a production folder (after due approvals from relevant authorities). In the case where these are copies, most IT organizations would require the file masking job or

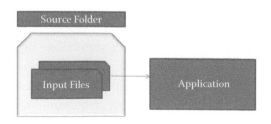

Figure 14.2 Sample standalone environment for an application.

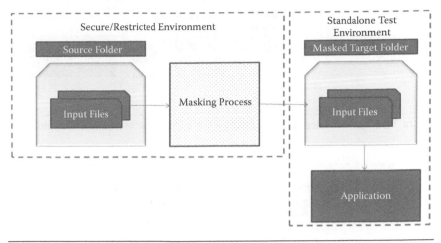

Figure 14.3   File masking pattern for a standalone test environment.

a postprocess job to delete the files. The masking process is executed in a restricted environment (similar to database masking) and access to the source folder as well as masking tool is controlled.

Most masking tools supporting file anonymization mask record by record. In case of an error, the new file generated with masked values will be deleted. This pattern can be extended to more input data sources in a standalone environment in a similar fashion where the anonymization process is executed from a secured environment and the test environment has only anonymized data sources available.

Integration Environment

In an integration environment, the application would be tested with input feeds or a message coming in from an upstream application and the application generates feeds or messages to a downstream application.

File Masking Pattern in an Integration Environment   Figure 14.4 shows a typical integrated environment where upstream and downstream applications communicate through feed files.

When upstream applications communicate to *AppToBeTested* (the application in scope for testing) through feed files, usage of the proxy input and proxy output folder comes into the picture. Thus the file masking pattern would be as shown in the diagram in Figure 14.5.

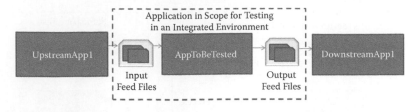

Figure 14.4   Sample integration environment where applications communicate using file feeds.

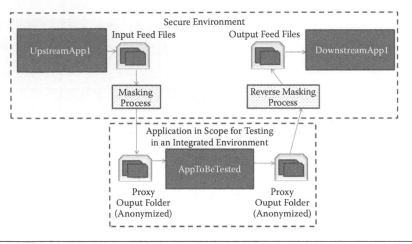

Figure 14.5   File masking pattern for an integration test environment.

The salient features of this pattern include:

- All sensitive data from input feeds would be desensitized through anonymization in a secure environment.
- The input feeds would arrive at the input folder and the anonymized feed files would be generated in a proxy input folder.
- The application in scope for testing (*AppToBeTested*) would be reconfigured to read from the proxy input folder instead of the input folder.
- The application in scope for testing (*AppToBeTested*) would be reconfigured to write into the proxy output folder instead of the output folder.
- Because the generated output feed file would contain masked values, the downstream application would have to reverse mask the feed files to test the output feed.

- Typically, input feed files would be anonymized using an encryption technique and a decryption technique (using the same key) would be used for reverse masking of the anonymized output files.

Message Masking Pattern in an Integration Environment In most application-to-application integration architectures, the communication between the applications happens in an asynchronous manner through messages using message queue middleware. A typical integrated environment where upstream and downstream applications communicate through messages in queues would be as shown in Figure 14.6.

When upstream applications communicate with the application in scope for testing through messages in queues, the use of proxy input and proxy output queues comes into the picture. Thus the masking pattern for messages in an integration environment would be as shown in Figure 14.7.

Figure 14.6 Sample integration environment where applications communicate using queued messages.

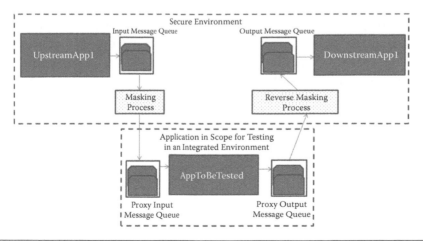

Figure 14.7 Pattern depicting masking of message in a queue in an integration test environment.

The salient features of this pattern include:

- All sensitive data from input messages would be desensitized through anonymization in a secure environment.
- The input messages from the upstream application would arrive at the input message queue and the anonymized messages would be generated in a proxy input queue.
- The application in scope for testing (*AppToBeTested*) would be reconfigured to read from the proxy input queue instead of the input queue.
- The application in scope for testing (*AppToBeTested*) would be reconfigured to write into the proxy output queue instead of the output queue.
- Because the generated output messages would contain masked values, the downstream application would have to reverse mask the messages to test the output messages.
- Typically, input messages would be anonymized using an encryption technique and (anonymized) output messages would be reverse masked using a decryption technique (using the same key).

Automated Integration Test Environment

An automated integration testing environment is a very "production-like" environment for testing. Here copies of the input files and messages keep coming in to the integration testing environment as and when they arrive in the production environment and they get processed by the application being tested. The output from this application is either archived or sent to downstream applications continuously. The benefits of this kind of environment are:

(a) Availability of production data for testing (in a masked format).
(b) Higher quality of testing and coverage of test cases.
(c) Lesser number of defects.
(d) Ease of replicating the scenario in case of any issue in production.
(e) Ease with which the cause of the issue can be determined. We can determine if the issue is because of bad data or whether it has to do with any application logic.

WHY IS AN AUTOMATED INTEGRATION TEST ENVIRONMENT NEEDED?

- Most enterprises have a time lag and a defined process for the application patch to move from a functional test/regression test environment to an integration test environment to a performance test environment to an acceptance test environment to production environments. Each of these testing environments may be shared or separate.
- These enterprises cannot afford the time lag to complete the end-to-end testing cycle from the functional test to acceptance test whenever a show-stopper bug is detected in production. This is especially true for critical applications in production, which process millions of transactions. For accelerating the time-to-production for a critical bug fix, continuously integrated environments are created and used as a preproduction test environment. The developers deploy their fix on this preproduction environment and testers certify the application in this environment before moving this into production to keep it running. Given that this environment is a near replica of the production environment, any issues arising out of the critical fix or hot-fix can be detected before moving to production.
- In order to ensure adherence to application development processes and release management processes of the organization, these critical fixes or hot-fixes are again bundled as part of the next subsequent release of the application and get tested through the functional test, integration test, and acceptance test cycles.

The challenges with this type of environment include:

(a) High amount of resource consumption.
(b) Higher amount of storage needed to save files.
(c) High-end servers needed for the environment, thereby increasing the cost.
(d) Higher cost and effort for maintaining the environment.

(e) Generally, most enterprises do not have the budget to provide a "near-production" environmentlike infrastructure for the test environment. In such a limited resource/budget scenario, a lot of time is spent in fixing infrastructure issues related to the test environment rather than testing the application.

Anonymization Pattern for an Automated Integration Test Environment As an example, let's look at an application, *AppinScope*, which:

- Receives feed files containing sensitive customer information and messages from upstream applications *UpstreamApp1* and *UpstreamApp2*, respectively.
- Processes this information and stores the sensitive information in table *customertableinscope* in database *AppInScopeDB1*.
- Generates a part of this information to the downstream application *DownstreamApp1* through an output feed file.

The data flow across the applications in a production environment would be as shown in Figure 14.8. For an automated integration test environment, the anonymization solution would be as shown in

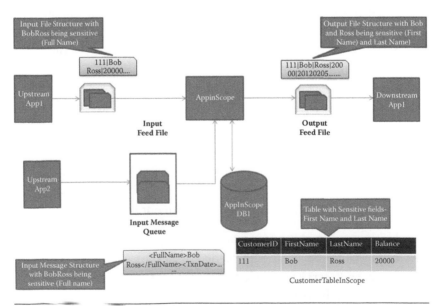

Figure 14.8 Dataflow for the given example in a production environment.

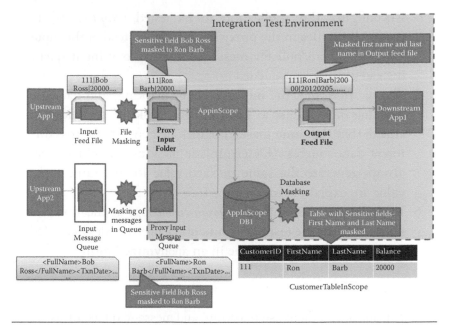

Figure 14.9 Anonymized solution for the given example for an automated integration test environment.

Figure 14.9. Thus the anonymization solution pattern for the above shown automated integration test environment would be:

1. Periodically mask the sensitive fields in the *AppInScopeDB1* (say once in a day or once in a week) using either of the static masking patterns (EAL or ELA).
2. Mask the input feed files arriving from upstream application *UpstreamApp1* (in a production environment) using a continuously running file masking process and generate the masked files in a proxy input folder. (A backend job can copy the production input files from *UpstreamApp1* into another folder from where these files can be masked and copied on to the proxy input folder.)
3. Mask the input messages arriving from upstream application *UpstreamApp2* (in a production environment) using a continuously running message masking process and generate the masked messages in a proxy input queue. (A backend job can copy the production input messages from *UpstreamApp2* into another message queue from where these messages can be masked and copied onto the proxy input queue.)

4. Reconfigure the application to be tested (*AppInScope*) to read/poll for files in the proxy input folder instead of the input folder and read/poll for messages in the proxy input queue instead of the input queue.

5. The file masking, the message queue masking, and database masking must all use a "deterministic masking" technique to ensure that the same masked names are generated across different data sources. (Deterministic masking techniques that always generate the same masked value for the same input value are explained in Chapter 16.)

6. In the current example, the *DownstreamApp1* application also needs to be in the test environment. Hence the files being fed into the system must also be in an anonymized form.

Controls to Be Enforced

1. File masking, database masking, and message queue masking jobs must not be accessible from the test environment.

2. The input folder and input queues must not be accessible in the test environment. These controls can be enforced using access control lists.

3. Only the anonymized database, proxy input folder, proxy input queue, and output folders may be accessible in the test environment.

Scaled-Down Integration Test Environment

A *scaled-down integration test environment* is an environment where the applications do not keep receiving input feeds or messages continuously. Rather, these feeds or messages are either created or a periodic dump from the production environment for a given date range is used for the integration test.

The benefits of having this environment for an integration test are:

(a) Integration can be conducted on a "scaled-down" production infrastructure.

(b) Testing files/feeds can be generated as and when needed.

(c) Lower cost and effort for maintaining this environment.

(d) Higher coverage of test cases as compared to a standalone test environment.

The challenges in using this environment for testing include:

(e) Lower quality of testing as compared to a continuously integrated environment.
(f) Although we get higher coverage of test cases as compared to a standalone test environment, some of the runtime test cases that can be tested in a continously integrated environment cannot be covered.
(g) Operational issues crop up, such as the need to prepare data or request data from production every time before testing.

For the same example as shown in the section on the continuously integrated environment, the anonymization solution for a scaled-down integration testing environment would be as shown in Figure 14.10.

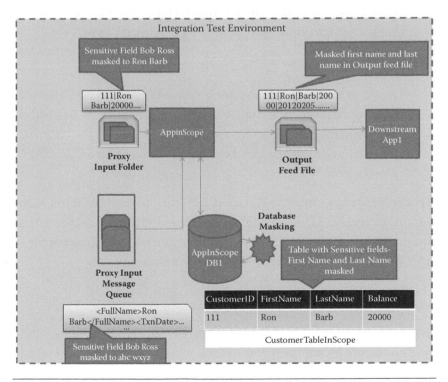

Figure 14.10 Anonymized solution for a scaled-down integration testing environment.

The anonymization solution pattern for the above shown periodically integrated test environment would be:

1. Periodically generate a database dump from the production environment for a date range and mask the sensitive fields in the *AppInScopeDB1* (say once in a day or once a week).
2. Create a test feed file matching the data in *AppInScopeDB1* in a test environment or request an input feed from production and mask the input feed files using an offline file-masking process.
3. Create test messages in the input queue matching fields in the *AppInScopeDB1* or request input messages from production and mask the messages using an offline message-masking process.
4. The file masking, the message queue masking, and database masking must all use a deterministic masking technique to ensure that the same masked names are generated across different data sources.
5. In the current example, the *DownstreamApp1* application also needs to be in the test environment. Hence the files being fed into the system must also be in an anonymized form.

Controls to Be Enforced

1. Database masking, file masking (if used), and message queue masking (if used) jobs must not be accessible from the test environment.
2. Only the anonymized database must be accessible in the test environment.

Generally, setting up an automated integration testing environment is more expensive than setting up a scaled-down integration testing environment, and a scaled-down integration testing environment is more expensive to set up than a standalone environment.

Conclusion

Once an application goes live on production, any nonproduction environment activities needed for the maintenance or enhancement of this application need to use anonymized data.

In order to ensure separation of concerns, different nonproduction environments such as unit test and development environment, functional and regression testing environment, integration test environment, user acceptance test, preproduction environment, or staging environments are needed and all these need anonymized data.

Testing can be performed in a standalone, automated integration test or a scaled down integration test environment. Static masking patterns (EAL, ELA), file masking patterns, and message masking patterns are all relevant to testing environments.

15

DATA FLOW PATTERNS
ACROSS ENVIRONMENTS

Points to Ponder

- How can data be moved from production to nonproduction environments while protecting the sensitivity of the data?
- How can files and messages be moved from production to nonproduction environments while protecting the sensitivity of the data?

This chapter is more of a continuation of the previous chapter. Whereas the previous chapter emphasized how database masking, file masking, and message queue masking patterns can be applied in different test environments based on the scope of the testing, in this chapter we look at how to design an anonymization solution for the flow of data from production to nonproduction environments along with a case study. To re-emphasize, once an application is live in production, all the nonproduction environments would need anonymized data.

**Flow of Data from Production Environment Databases
to Nonproduction Environment Databases**

Databases used for different types of testing need different volumes of anonymized data. Figure 15.1 suggests a pattern for flow of anonymized data from a production environment.

The salient features of the pattern include:

1. Creation of a gold copy of production data with sensitive fields anonymized. The gold copy is an exact copy of the production data as of a particular cut-off date with the sensitive fields anonymized. The gold copy is periodically refreshed (using incremental masking) weekly or daily as per

the frequency of the usage of the preproduction and performance test environments.

2. These anonymized data can be copied from the gold copy to preproduction and performance test environments. Generally the preproduction and performance test environments are near-production in nature. Hence the database here can be a copy of the latest gold copy and these databases can be refreshed as per a defined frequency.

Enterprises must ensure that data need to go through an anonymization test before they can move to nonproduction environments. (Courtesy of Jophy Joy)

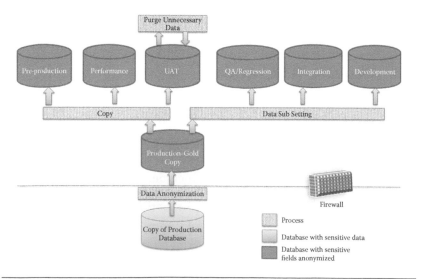

Figure 15.1 Anonymization solution for flow of data from production environment to nonproduction environment.

CHALLENGES OF USING
ANONYMIZED DATA FOR UAT

In many organizations, the business or acceptance users refuse to test with any type of data that are in an encrypted format if they are not so in production systems. It is thus necessary to ensure that anonymization techniques generate "realistic data" and use of encryption techniques to generate anonymized data is minimized as far as possible.

3. The UAT environment needs only a specific set of data that varies as per the business user's requirement. Some organizations copy the gold copy of the data and purge the unwanted data here instead of subsetting the data.
4. In order to save on infrastructure costs, most IT departments provide only a scaled-down infrastructure for the QA/regression test, integration, and development environments. Subsetting anonymized data (using the data subsetting module that generally comes bundled with most popular data anonymization tools) from the gold copy helps ensure that:
    • The data are just enough for the limited storage space available in these environments.
    • Enough data for the relevant test cases are available.
    • The data set available for testing includes all related records.

Controls Followed

The database anonymization jobs are executed in a secure environment within the firewall and only anonymized data are accessible from any nonproduction environments.

**Movement of Anonymized Files from Production
Environment to Nonproduction Environments**

Let's take an example of an application *AppInScope* receiving input files from an upstream application *UpstreamApp1* as shown in Figure 15.2.

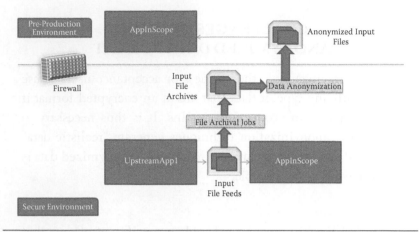

Figure 15.2 Movement of anonymized files from production environment to nonproduction environment.

This pattern comprises additional anonymization jobs in a secure environment and replication of the folder structure as a source of anonymized file input for nonproduction environments. For all nonproduction purposes, the input files will be either retrieved from the archive folder or copied from the source folder (where the upstream applications generate the files) and anonymized by continuously running jobs. These jobs generate the anonymized files in a target folder that would serve as the anonymized file repository (which will also follow the same naming convention as the production environment).

The environment-specific characteristics and requirements are:

1. *Production environment*: In most legacy applications, the archived input files (from an upstream application) in a production environment generally follow a datewise folder naming convention. Thus all the input files processed by the application (*AppInScope*) on a particular day are stored in that date's folder. The filenames generally contain the timestamp when the file was generated by the upstream application.

2. *Preproduction Environment*: Only the preproduction environment is a continuously integrated environment needing all the input files processed by the production application.

3. *Performance Test Environment*: The performance test environment can have a copy of the anonymized input files from the anonymized input file repository or archive.
4. *Integration Test Environment*: For the integration test environment, the input files can be created or a specified file from the anonymized input file repository/archive can be used whenever we test the application. There is no continuous need for input files.
5. *System and Regression Test Environment*: System and regression test environments need only *created test* files. If necessary, the anonymized input file can be used from the anonymized input file repository/archive whenever needed. If the file is too big, only a subset of the records can be retained and rest of the data in the file can be purged.
6. *Development Environment*: Development environments also need only created test files. If necessary, the anonymized input file can be used from the anonymized input file repository/archive whenever needed. If the file is too big, only a subset of the records can be retained and rest of the data in the file can be purged.

Controls

Only the anonymized folder is accessible from nonproduction environments. The anonymization jobs as well as the original input files are not accessible from nonproduction environments.

Masked Environment for Integration Testing—Case Study

Let's take an example of how an anonymized integration environment can be implemented for an application with multiple input data sources that contain sensitive data (which is typical of many banking applications) as elaborated in the following case study. See Figure 15.3.

The application that needs to be tested in an integration environment, *AppToBeTested*, receives input from two upstream applications *UpstreamApp1* and *UpstreamApp2*.

- *UpstreamApp1* sends feed files to *AppToBeTested* containing sensitive customer data.

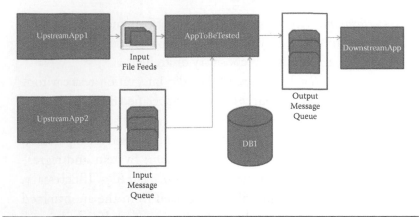

Figure 15.3   Integration architecture for the application to be tested with anonymized data.

- *UpstreamApp2* communicates to *AppToBeTested* through messages in the message queue and these messages also contain sensitive customer data.
- *AppToBeTested* processes these data, stores them in its database *DB1*, and also sends out messages to *DownstreamApp1* through an output message queue.
- The sensitive customer data are all related and the application *AppToBeTested* maintains the relational integrity between the data sources while processing these data.

Objectives of the Anonymization Solution

- In order to test the *AppToBeTested* application in an integrated environment, sensitive customer data need to be masked in *DB1*, input feed files, and input message queues.
- We need to ensure that masking does not break the relational integrity of the sensitive customer data across these data sources.

Key Anonymization Solution Principles

When the scope of the testing is limited to only *AppToBeTested*, the following principles are followed as part of the anonymization process:

- All sensitive data from input feeds must be desensitized through anonymization.

- The related fields from multiple input sources must be anony-mized using the same tool, the same masking technique, and potentially the same encryption key.
- All output data feeds will be in masked format. If the down-stream application needs to process these data, it should use the same masking technique for its anonymization needs and preferably the same tool.
- If not, the masked data would have to be unmasked and masked again using the tool used by the downstream application.

Solution Implementation

Detailed Sensitivity Analysis The first step in the anonymization process is to conduct a sensitivity analysis on the entire application *AppToBeTested*. This exercise would provide:

- A list of the fields needed to be anonymized in the database *DB1*
- The list of sensitive fields in the input feed files
- The list of sensitive fields in the messages in the input message queue
- The list of sensitive fields in the messages in the output queue
- The mapping (or the relation) between the sensitive fields in the database *DB1*, input feed files, and input messages

Anonymization Technique Selection   Here we identify the techniques that can be applied for anonymization of the sensitive fields. The key considerations here include the following:

Relational Integrity Preservation   Given that referential integrity preservation across data sources typically is maintained by the appli-cations themselves, it is imperative that any anonymization fit into the integrated solution allows for the implicit relationship to remain as is. Thus, by having the related fields across the data sources use the same anonymization technique (typically encryption) and same encryp-tion key, the anonymization solution can ensure relational integrity between these fields (i.e., CustFirstName in *DB1*, the field follow-ing the first delimiter in the input file that refers to the Customer

First Name, and the value of the <CustFirstName> tag in the input message all use the same technique).

Testing Scope   If the scope of the testing stops with just ensuring that the output messages are generated, we do not need to worry about de-anonymization of the sensitive fields that were masked. We just need to ensure that the related sensitive fields in the input data sources and database *DB1* use a deterministic masking technique.

If the scope of the testing is to ensure that the output messages are processed by the downstream application *DownstreamApp*, we will need to ensure that the fields in the output message queue that are related to the anonymized fields in the database *DB1*, the input messages, or the input files are made available to the *DownstreamApp* in the format expected by the downstream application. This has two possibilities:

(a) If the *DownstreamApp* uses a different anonymization solution or tool, we can use only encryption as the anonymization technique for the related sensitive fields in *DB1* and input data sources and will need to decrypt the related fields in the output message using the same key (which was used for encryption of the sensitive fields in the input data sources or database).

(b) If the *DownstreamApp* uses the same anonymization solution, then there is no need to decrypt the related fields in the output messages and they can be passed through as is. Here any deterministic masking technique is sufficient for anonymizing the related sensitive fields in input data sources and *DB1*.

In this case, let's assume that *DownstreamApp* uses a different tool for masking in an integrated environment. Hence we use encryption to mask the sensitive fields and decryption using the same key before sending the message to *DownstreamApp*.

Anonymization Environment Design

Here are the questions we need to consider as part of the anonymization environment design:

- Which are the nonproduction environments where anonymization is needed? The answer to this question helps in designing the flow of anonymized data across environments.

- Which are the types of tests conducted for the application and in which environments? Do multiple tests share the same environment? Does the environment need to be "integrated" or "standalone"? If the environment needs to be integrated, should it be automated integration or should it be a scaled-down integration test environment?

These are important questions to be answered given that each type of environment would need different components of the anonymization solution. For the current case study, the different types of tests performed are the regression test, functional test, integration test, performance test, and UAT (acceptance test) and the environments available are a regression/functional test environment, integration test environment, preproduction, and UAT environment. In addition, the organization has an environment for training users and hence would need a training environment.

Table 15.1 provides the details of the purpose and outlines the constraints of the environment as well as the anonymization components needed for each environment.

Anonymization Solution

The anonymization solution would comprise the following jobs (processes):

- Batch job to anonymize the sensitive fields in the database *DB1*
- Batch job to anonymize the input feed files
- Batch job to anonymize the input messages in the queue
- Batch job to de-anonymize the output queued messages (before being fed into the anonymization solution of *DownstreamApp*)
- Miscellaneous other batch jobs such as data subsetting jobs, file archival/deletion jobs, queued messages archival/deletion jobs, jobs for copying anonymized data across different test environments, jobs for copying anonymized files across different environments, and jobs for copying anonymized messages across message queues in different environments

Most organizations introduce the anonymization solution into each of the test environments gradually. The solution is introduced taking

Table 15.1 Anonymization Components Needed for Each Environment

ENVIRONMENT	TYPE OF ENVIRONMENT	ANONYMIZATION SOLUTION COMPONENTS REQUIRED	COMMENTS
Regression test/ functional test environment	Standalone	Database masking.	For testing processing of feed files and messages, the files and messages may be manufactured with data matching the anonymized data in the database.
Integration test environment	Scaled-down integration environment	Database masking + (file masking) anonymized files (stripped down to only necessary records)/ messages can be retrieved from preproduction repository/archive or file masking and queued message masking jobs may be run periodically if file/ message is retrieved from archives).	Files and messages from production may be needed only periodically. Whenever we need them, we can request the data team/ production IT team to retrieve these files/messages from the archives. Or these files/ messages can be manufactured.
Preproduction environment	Automated integration environment	Database masking + file masking + queued message masking. Database masking job will be run periodically, say once a day, whereas file and queued message masking jobs will be running continuously.	Archival/deletion jobs for purging the files will need to be run to ensure that the storage is freed up after a few days.
Performance environment	Standalone or integrated	Database masking + (file masking) + (message queue masking).	Depends on the objective of the performance testing. If the objective is to test with large volumes of data, then only database masking is sufficient. If, however, files and messages are also needed, then masking components of files and queued messages are also needed.
UAT	Standalone	Database masking.	Files and messages are generally manufactured. Care should be taken that anonymized data are realistic enough for the business users.

Table 15.1 (*Continued*)   Anonymization Components Needed for Each Environment

ENVIRONMENT	TYPE OF ENVIRONMENT	ANONYMIZATION SOLUTION COMPONENTS REQUIRED	COMMENTS
Training	Standalone	Database masking.	Because the end users of the application would be interacting only with the user interface of the application, this environment typically does not need input files or queued messages.

one environment at a time. This gradual approach helps alleviate the risk in the impact of change in behavior of the application due to introduction of the anonymization solution. The least risky environment (and most often, the test environment that is most frequently used), where the anonymization solution would be introduced, would be the System/Regression test environment.

Anonymization Solution for the Regression Test/
Functional Testing Environment

The anonymization solution for this environment would be as shown in the diagram in Figure 15.4. The scope of this testing involves only testing the functionality of the application. Any integration needed here is mocked up. Thus input files and input messages are also manufactured data. This is a standalone environment. The need for realistic data (production data) is only from a database perspective. Thus the anonymization solution here comprises only database masking as of a particular date. Given the limited resources available, the data are most often a subset of the production data with sensitive fields anonymized.

Once the anonymization solution has reached a steady state and testers are comfortable in testing with anonymized data, an anonymization solution for an integrated environment is introduced.

Anonymization Solution for an Integration Testing Environment

This environment also has a scaled-down integration infrastructure. Any files needed for testing are retrieved from the production environment after anonymization only at the time of testing. Anonymization is not a continuous need here. The solution would be an anonymized

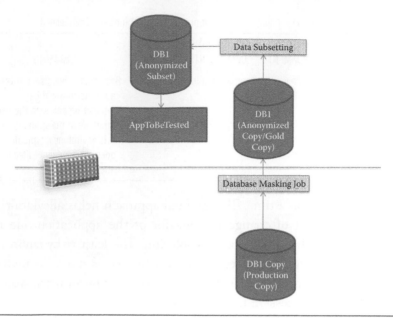

Figure 15.4 Anonymization solution for the regression test/functional testing environment.

database production dump (data subsets) for a particular date apart from anonymized input files and input queued messages from production for the same date. Integration with the downstream system is not tested here and as long as the output feed file is generated with the expected records, the application is treated as having behaved as per expectations. The anonymization solution is shown in Figure 15.5.

Anonymization Solution for UAT Environment

User acceptance testers are generally business users and are highly reluctant to test with anonymized data. The objective of UAT is to ensure that the application behaves as expected and rarely covers integration testing. The anonymization solution for UAT would be the same as the regression testing environment solution (standalone environment) and will thus require only database masking. Care should be taken that none of the sensitive fields is masked using gibberish data or is encrypted.

Anonymization Solution for Preproduction Environment

Given the criticality associated with a preproduction or hot-fix environment, this is the last of the environments where anonymization

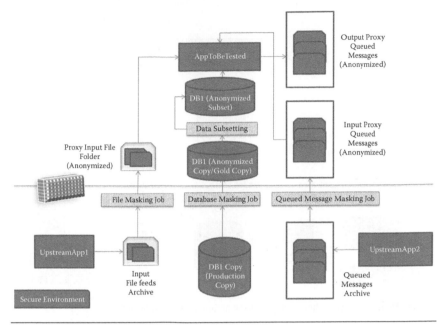

Figure 15.5 Anonymization solution for the integration testing environment.

is taken up. This is a replica of the production environment and any anonymization solution would require the anonymized data, files, and messages to be available in the environment with as little delay as possible from the production environment. Thus the database would be incrementally anonymized at least once a day and the file and queued message masking jobs would run continuously. Additional jobs such as file/message purging/archiving will be needed to ensure that the environment is cleaned of unwanted files. Figure 15.6 depicts the anonymization solution for a preproduction environment. As the downstream application uses a different anonymization solution, it is necessary to unmask the output messages. Care should be taken that the testers do not have access to unmasked messages and the unmasking jobs. These jobs must be executed in a secure environment given that they will need to use the same key used for encrypting the messages.

Anonymization Solution for Performance Test Environment

A performance test environment needs a high volume of data/files/messages. Based on whether the application is being tested for

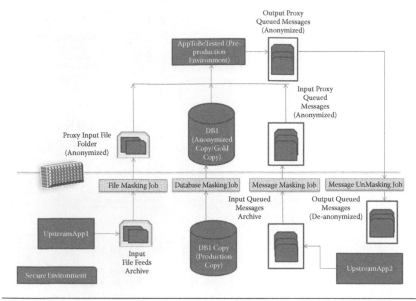

Figure 15.6 Anonymization solution for the preproduction environment.

performance when a large amount of data is being processed or when large files or numbers of messages are being processed, the anonymization solution can be a standalone database masking solution (without data subsetting) or can be combined with file masking and queued message masking.

Anonymization Solution for Training Environment

This would be very similar to an anonymization solution for a UAT environment.

Reusing the Anonymization Infrastructure across the Various Environments

Once the anonymization solution is in a steady state across environments, the reusable anonymization infrastructure across environments would be as shown in Figure 15.7.

Let's denote the anonymized input folder source as *F*, the anonymized gold copy of production data to be *D*, the anonymized input message queue source as *IQ*, the output messages generated by the application in the preproduction environment to be *OQ*, and the job for unmasking the messages in the output proxy queue to be *JU*.

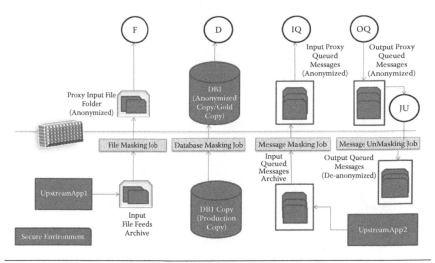

Figure 15.7   Reusable data anonymization infrastructure.

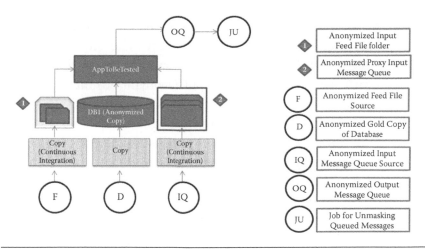

Figure 15.8   Leveraging the reusable data anonymization infrastructure for a preproduction environment.

Leveraging the Reusable Data Anonymization Infrastructure

How can the preproduction environment leverage the reusable data anonymization infrastructure?

The reusable infrastructure would provide anonymization data to the preproduction (and if necessary performance test environment) as shown in Figure 15.8.

How can the integration (scaled-down) environment leverage the reusable data anonymization infrastructure?

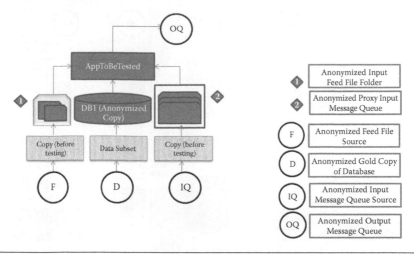

Figure 15.9 Leveraging the reusable data anonymization infrastructure for an integration test environment.

The integration test environment would leverage the reusable data anonymization infrastructure as shown in the diagram in Figure 15.9. In this environment, testing ends with the generation of output (anonymized) messages in the queue and we don't further pass the output messages in the message queue to an unmasking job (JU). Only a subset of the messages from IQ, a subset of files from F, and a subset of data from D are needed for this environment.

How can the regression test and functional test environment leverage the reusable data anonymization infrastructure?

The regression test/functional test environment would leverage the reusable anonymization infrastructure as shown in Figure 15.10. The UAT and training environments may need a separate database anonymization instance only if an encryption technique is used for anonymizing any field in the database; otherwise the existing anonymization infrastructure can be leveraged and the anonymization approach for the UAT and training environments would be the same as that of the regression and functional test environments. In this environment tool, the testing ends with generation of output (anonymized) messages in the output message queue and we don't further pass the output messages in the message queue to an unmasking job.

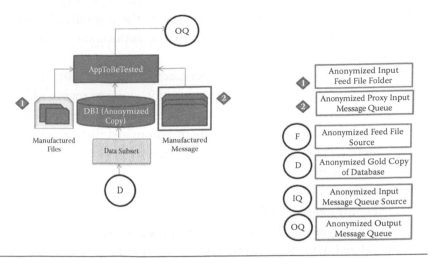

Figure 15.10 Leveraging the reusable data anonymization infrastructure for a regression test and functional test environment.

Conclusion

When designing for data anonymization, it is necessary:

- To understand the environments that would need anonymized data given that different environments have different needs of anonymized data for the same application
- To understand the as-is flow of data from the production environment to the nonproduction environments given that the anonymization solution must fit in with the as-is flow of data from production to nonproduction environments

Anonymization Environment Design

The data sources of the application that contain sensitive data can be anonymized and stored as a centralized repository of anonymized data. This repository will be a copy of the production data with sensitive fields anonymized, will serve as the source of anonymized data to all nonproduction environments hosting the application, and will be periodically refreshed.

For an application with database, files, and messages (in queues) as the sensitive input data source, there will be a gold copy of anonymized data for anonymized database needs, an anonymized file store for file needs, and an anonymized message store (queue) for all

message queue needs and these will serve as the centralized repositories for the anonymized data needs of the application in different
environments.

From an anonymized database perspective, functional/regression
test environment, scaled-down integration environments, UAT,
and training environment will have data subset from the gold copy
whereas a preproduction environment/automated integration test
environment and performance test environment would need a copy of
the entire anonymized database.

Other than a preproduction environment, other environments do
not need continuous refreshing of files or message queues. The sensitive files/messages can be created or a subset of files/messages from
the centralized data store can be taken for a specific date range.

16
DATA ANONYMIZATION TECHNIQUES

Points to Ponder

- What are the basic anonymization techniques?
- What are the derivative anonymization techniques?
- When should these techniques be used?

Data anonymization techniques help in removing the information content from the data. These techniques can be statistical, algorithmic, or custom built and must ensure that the data type of the field remains unchanged: that is, the masked value and original value must belong to the same data type.

As shown in Figure 16.1, the basic data anonymization techniques are: cryptographic, substitution, character masking, nulling out, date variance, number variance, and shuffling. Figure 16.1 depicts that cryptographic and substitution techniques can be leveraged for repeatable, nonrepeatable, partial, and conditional masking of data and character masking; date variance and number variance can be leveraged for partial and conditional masking of data; and nulling out technique can be leveraged for conditional masking of data.

DETERMINISTIC OR REPEATABLE MASKING

When the same masked value is always generated by a technique, it is a case of repeatable or deterministic masking. The repeatability is agnostic of the data store type (file/database and message queue) and database technology, e.g., when "King" is always masked to "Brad" irrespective of the database technology or the type of data store.

Deterministic or repeatable masking techniques help whenever we need to ensure the preservation of relational integrity across multiple data stores.

Which masking technique should be chosen? (Courtesy of Jophy Joy)

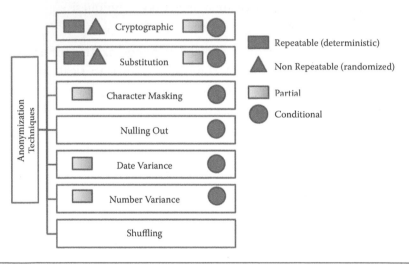

Figure 16.1 Basic anonymization techniques.

Basic Anonymization Techniques

Substitution

What Is Substitution? Here the input (unmasked) data are randomly or always replaced by substitute data. The data type of the input data can be numeric or alpha numeric or can also be a date. Substitution can be applied on the complete input data or on specific portions of the input data. This technique can also be applied based on conditions. Table 16.1 depicts an application of substitution technique where each character in the input (unmasked) data is replaced randomly by another character to generate the masked value.

Table 16.1   Random Substitution

	FIELD VALUE	COMMENTS
Unmasked (input value)	LONDON01	Here the data type and length of the field are preserved. The substitute characters are generated randomly using this algorithm.
Masked (output value)	ABMEQD12	In this example, the character "O" in "LONDON01" is substituted every time with different characters, namely "B" and "Q." Similarly, the character "N" is replaced differently each time with "M" and "D."

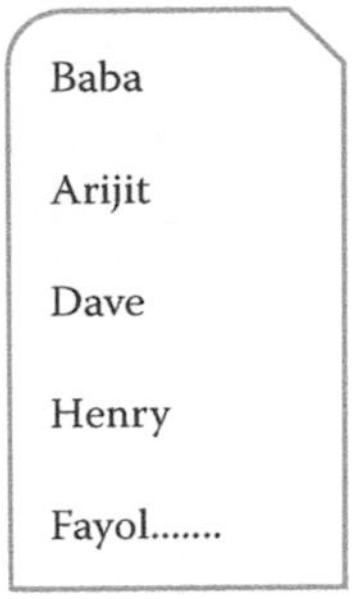

Baba

Arijit

Dave

Henry

Fayol.......

Figure 16.2   External file containing the list of names.

When Should This Technique Be Used?   This technique is useful when the type and format of the masked data need to be preserved and we don't need to worry about the masked data being realistic. When we need the masked data to be realistic, we look at a variant of this technique, which is "word substitution" or "lookup substitution" as explained below.

What Are the Variants of Substitution?

Word Substitution or Lookup Technique: In this technique, an external file or repository contains a list of values. The data to be masked will be replaced with a value from the external file or repository. Let us assume that the external file or repository has the list of names as shown in Figure 16.2. Table 16.2 depicts how the Word substitution technique works. The value Aster in the sensitive data store is replaced by the value in the external file.

When Should This Technique Be Used?   This technique is usually used when masked data need to be realistic, especially for names. The disadvantage of this technique is that for masking a large data set, a large list of values in the external file is also needed.

Table 16.2 Lookup Substitution

	FIELD VALUE	COMMENTS
Unmasked (input data)	Aster	Here the data length is not necessarily preserved. Based on the support provided by the tool, the name is selected from the file randomly or deterministically.
Masked (output data)	Dave	

Table 16.3 Customer Transaction Table before Anonymization

TRANSACTION ID	ACCOUNT NUMBER	TRANSACTION DATE	TRANSACTION AMOUNT	BALANCE
100001	6001298791	23-Mar-2011	2000	10000
100002	6001298891	2-Feb-2012	200	7800
100003	6011398801	1-Mar-2012	788	9880
100004	6014546781	10-Oct-2011	2055	2990

Table 16.4 Customer Transaction Table after Anonymization Using Shuffling

TRANSACTION ID	ACCOUNT NUMBER	TRANSACTION DATE	TRANSACTION AMOUNT	BALANCE
100001	6014546781	23-Mar-2011	2000	10000
100002	6001298791	2-Feb-2012	200	7800
100003	6001298891	1-Mar-2012	788	9880
100004	6011398801	10-Oct-2011	2055	2990

Shuffling

Shuffling involves the rearrangement of the data within the same column across different rows in a table as shown in Table 16.3, where the *AccountNumber* is a sensitive field that will be anonymized using the shuffling technique as shown in Table 16.4.

Thus the shuffling of the *AccountNumber* column ensures that the account number is not associated with the account balance or transaction amount. This rearrangement can be random in nature, but must ensure that the column data cannot be correlated with the other columns to infer the personal data.

When Should This Technique Be Used? Shuffling preserves the data type as it does not involve introduction of new data. It is a relatively simple technique to implement. Shuffling is more effective when applied on a table with a large number of records as compared to a table with fewer records. With a small data set (number of records), it is easy to trace back the original sensitive data and hence shuffling should not be used on a data set with a small number of records.

What Are the Variations of the Shuffling Technique? Group shuffling is a variation of the shuffling technique. Here a group of columns are shuffled together. Table 16.5 depicts the anonymization of a CustomerAddress Table where the objective is to ensure that the addresses are realistic but de-identified.

Group shuffling can be used to de-identify the Address (2), State, and Zip Code fields from the Customer ID field. After using Group Shuffling, the Customer Address table would look like that in Table 16.6. In this example, Waltham, being in Massachusetts (MA) with zip code 02455, and Phoenix, being in AZ with zip code 85097, would give an impression to the end user that the address is a true address although it is actually not so.

When Should This Technique Be Used? When grouped information needs to be anonymized together, as in the case of Address being split into different columns such as Address (2), Country, State, and Zip Code, this technique can be used. The objective is to have realistic data for testing but still ensure that the address is fictitious. As with shuffling, this technique is effective only on a large data set.

Table 16.5 Customer Address Table before Anonymization

CUSTOMER ID	ADDRESS 1	ADDRESS 2	STATE	ZIP CODE
100001	606, Edison Square	Phoenix	AZ	85097
100002	202, Thomas St	Edison	NJ	08817
100003	4, King Street	Waltham	MA	02455
100004	555, Jefferson Plaza	Chicago	IL	60604

Table 16.6 Customer Address Table after Group Shuffling

CUSTOMER ID	ADDRESS 1	ADDRESS 2	STATE	ZIP CODE
100001	606, Edison Square	Waltham	MA	02455
100002	202, Thomas St	Chicago	IL	60604
100003	4, King Street	Phoenix	AZ	85097
100004	555, Jefferson Plaza	Edison	NJ	08817

Number Variance

This statistical technique involves the generation of a number (or variation of the existing unmasked number) between a set of upper limit and lower limit as specified by the user. If the generated number after the variation is beyond the range (i.e., more than the upper limit or lesser than the lower limit), the anonymized number would be the same as the upper or lower limit. Let us take an example of a Customer Deposit table as shown in Table 16.7.

Applying the number variance technique to the Deposit column in the Customer Deposit table with 15,000 and 25,000 being the lower and upper limits and the increment (i.e., arithmetic operator is "+") number being specified as 1000 would result in the Deposit column having anonymized values as shown in Table 16.8.

Randomized Number Variance Technique   The number variance technique can be further strengthened by keeping the selection of arithmetic operator or function (or statistical variation mechanism) dependent on the generation of a random number.

Let us take the same example as above where the existing data set to be anonymized is the Deposit column in the Customer Deposit table with values as shown in Table 16.9.

Table 16.7 Customer Deposit Table before Anonymization

CUSTOMER ID	DEPOSIT
100001	25,000
100002	13,000
100003	20,000
100004	18,000

Table 16.8 Customer Deposit Table after Anonymization

CUSTOMER ID	DEPOSIT
100001	25,000
100002	15,000
100003	21,000
100004	19,000

Table 16.9 Customer Deposit
Table before Anonymization

CUSTOMER ID	DEPOSIT
100001	25,000
100002	13,000
100003	20,000
100004	18,000

Table 16.10 Customer Deposit Table
after Anonymization

CUSTOMER ID	DEPOSIT	RANDOM NUMBER
100001	25,000	6
100002	15,000	3
100003	21,000	7
100004	17,000	2

Let us have the upper limit as 25,000 and lower limit as 15,000 and the user specified rule being that if generated random number is between 0 and 4, the number will be decremented by 1000 and if generated random number is between 5 and 9, the number will be incremented by 1000.

Applying randomized number variance on the above data set using the above specifications would result in Table 16.10. Most anonymization tools supporting this technique allow the user to specify upper and lower limits, the variation number, and the arithmetic operator rule.

When Should This Technique Be Used?   This technique is useful in:

- HR systems, for masking the salary of the employees within a certain range of salary scale
- Banking systems, when applied on customer deposits, balances, etc.

As the name suggests, this technique is used only on numeric data.

Date Variance

This statistical technique involves generation of a date (or variation of the existing unmasked date) between a set of upper and lower limits

Table 16.11 Customer Table before Anonymization

CUSTOMER ID	DATE_OF_BIRTH
100001	1-Jan-1978
100002	30-Sep-1974
100003	30-Sep-1978
100004	1-Oct-1980

Table 16.12 Customer Table after Anonymization

CUSTOMER ID	DATE_OF_BIRTH
100001	31-Jan-1978
100002	1-Jan-1975
100003	30-Oct-1978
100004	1-Jan-1979

as specified by the user. If the generated data after the variation is beyond the range, the anonymized date would be the same as the upper or lower limits.

Let us look at an example of applying the date variance technique on the Date_of_Birth column as shown in Table 16.11. Let the upper limit be specified as 1-Jan-1979, lower limit as 1-Jan-1975, and increment as 30 days. The resultant masked Customer table would be as shown in Table 16.12.

Randomized Date Variance Technique The date variance technique can be further strengthened by keeping the arithmetic operator or function dependent on the generation of a random number or date. Most anonymization tools supporting this technique allow the user to specify upper and lower limits as well as the duration by which the date field must be varied and the arithmetic operator rule.

When Should This Technique Be Used? This technique is useful in:

- HR systems, for masking the date of birth or date of joining of the employees within a certain range of dates
- Banking systems, when applied on customer birth dates, etc.

As the name suggests, this technique is used only on date-type data.

Nulling out   This is a simple technique of replacing a column with sensitive values with null values.

When Should This Technique Be Used?   This technique is useful only for a limited set of scenarios. One of the limitations of this technique is that this technique cannot be used on columns that are not nullable: for example, replacing the "Gender" (Male/Female) column in EmployeeMaster or CustomerMaster table in an employee database or customer database with null values. A specific use is to replace the "Comments" field in the table with null values.

What Are the Variations of This Technique?

Character Replacement Technique   Instead of null, any other character such as space (" "), "Y", "N", and so on can be used as the replacement value. For example, if a background check database is being tested, the "Involved_in_Criminal_Activities" field would be a sensitive field. If this column contained a mix of "Y" and "N", we could have the entire column replaced with the value "N" in order to protect the privacy of those whose background check details have been stored in the database.

Another example is to de-identify disabled employees by setting a percentage of the employees in a region to "Y" and the rest to "N" as shown in Table 16.13. One of the anonymization strategy options would be to shuffle the region and then have 10% of the employees

Table 16.13   Unmasked Employee Table

EMPLOYEE ID	REGION	DISABLED
100001	Midwest	Y
100002	Midwest	N
100003	Midwest	Y
100004	Midwest	Y
100005	Northeast	N
100006	Northeast	Y
100007	Midwest	N
100008	Midwest	N
100009	Northwest	N
100010	Midwest	N
100011	Midwest	N
100012	Midwest	N
100013	Midwest	N
100014	Northwest	N

in a particular region character replaced to "Y". Shuffling the region would have results as shown in Table 16.14.

After setting the Disability flag to "Y" for 10% of the employees in a particular region, the anonymized table would be as shown in Table 16.15.

Table 16.14   Shuffled Employee Table

EMPLOYEE ID	REGION	DISABLED
100001	Northeast	Y
100002	Midwest	N
100003	Northeast	Y
100004	Midwest	Y
100005	Northwest	N
100006	Midwest	Y
100007	Northwest	N
100008	Midwest	N
100009	Midwest	N
100010	Midwest	N
100011	Midwest	N
100012	Midwest	N
100013	Midwest	N
100014	Midwest	N

Table 16.15   Anonymized Employee Table with 10% of the Employees Disabled

EMPLOYEE ID	REGION	DISABLED
100001	Northeast	N
100002	Midwest	N
100003	Northeast	Y
100004	Midwest	N
100005	Northwest	N
100006	Midwest	N
100007	Northwest	N
100008	Midwest	Y
100009	Midwest	N
100010	Midwest	N
100011	Midwest	N
100012	Midwest	N
100013	Midwest	N
100014	Midwest	N

Removal of Data In certain cases, it is okay to remove the data themselves. For example, when creating a gold copy of the employee database for testing, the organization can mandate that all data about employee performance in the "Comments" column has to be removed.

Conditional Nulling out or Removal Technique This technique is about nulling out or removing data when a certain condition is met. For example, removing all data in the "Comments" column when the "Customer Complaint" column has a value "Y."

Character Masking

This is one of the most popular techniques used in data masking. This technique replaces the entire value or partial value with characters such as X, *, &, and so on. The length of the masked value remains unchanged.

When Should This Technique Be Used? This technique is used for masking credit card numbers. For example, credit card number 4455 3230 0010 5169 can be partially anonymized with the character X and the masked value would be XXXX XXXX XXXX 5169.

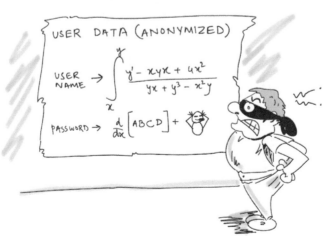

The safety of masking. (Courtesy of Jophy Joy)

Cryptographic Techniques[1]

Cryptography typically involves the usage of terms including plain text, cipher text, cipher, and symmetric key, among others, and these have been described in the glossary.

Cryptographic techniques are relevant for data anonymization when confidentiality and integrity of data are the key considerations as opposed to anonymized data being realistic. Thus cryptographic techniques are more relevant for dynamic masking and integration test environment requirements as compared to static test environments.

What Are the Variations of Cryptographic Techniques? Cryptographic techniques can be classified into symmetric key techniques, public key techniques, and message digest techniques (see Figure 16.3).

Symmetric Key Techniques This technique involves use of the same key to anonymize the data as well as de-anonymize the data. Cryptographically, the original data are called "plain text" and after "encryption" with a "key," these data become "cipher text." See Figure 16.4.

Encryption can be achieved by use of the following techniques.

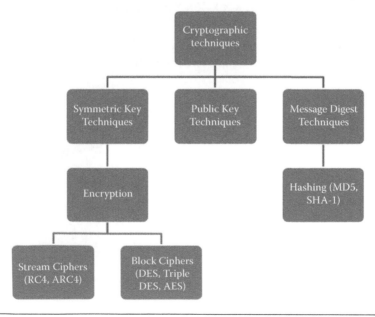

Figure 10.3 Cryptographic techniques.

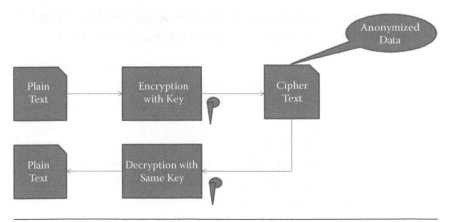

Figure 16.4   Symmetric key cryptography techniques used for anonymization.

Stream Cipher   Here every plain text bit is combined with a key stream bit to arrive at a cipher bit. Stream cipher generation techniques, although popular, are vulnerable to attacks such as "known plain text attack."

One of the popular algorithms used for generating stream cipher is alleged RC4.

Block Cipher   Here the data are broken into blocks of bits (say 64 bits) and then each block is encrypted. The DES (data encryption standard) algorithm and Triple DES are two implementations of the block cipher technique.

- DES uses a 56-bit symmetric key for encrypting the 64-bit plain text input blocks.
- Triple DES is a more secure algorithm where the 64-bit block of data is encrypted three times with three different keys.
- AES (advanced encryption standard) is a relatively newer algorithm that adheres to the U.S. NIST 2001 Standard where data are processed in larger blocks of 128 bits. The symmetric keys used in AES for encryption can be 128, 192, or 256 bit keys. This algorithm has now replaced DES.

When Should Symmetric Key Techniques Be Used?   The encryption technique is relevant for the following anonymization scenarios:

- Production environment dynamic masking scenarios

- Integration test environment where the application being tested needs to receive sensitive data from upstream applications

The high relevance of encryption to the above scenarios arises from the fact that the data have to be transmitted without the risk of being tampered with and the confidentiality of these data has to be ensured during transmission.

Encryption is typically chosen in any scenario where there is a need to retrieve the original data (de-anonymized data) back as part of the data flow. As already mentioned, dynamic masking and integration testing are examples of such scenarios.

Before the advent of popular data anonymization tools, encryption had been the most popular technique used for anonymizing sensitive data. Despite the overwhelming popularity of encryption as a technique for data anonymization, there are the following drawbacks:

- It is not useful when anonymized data need to be realistic.
- The key used for encrypting data must also be access controlled, restricted to limited users, and stored securely. Key management overheads need to be taken into account when planning for usage of this technique.

Public Key Techniques   Public key techniques that involve the use of a public key–private key pair and involve algorithms such as RSA are not much used in the world of data anonymization. Hence these techniques are not discussed further.

Message Digest Techniques   Message digest techniques involve the use of a hashing function that generates a fixed-length hash string output for an arbitrary length input message.

Key Objectives behind the Design of Message Digest Algorithms
- *Irreversibility*: The input value that is to be anonymized must not be retrievable from the output hash.
- *Collision-free*: A hash value must ensure that there are no collisions: that is, two different inputs can at no stage produce the same hash value.
- *Deterministic*: A hashing function must produce the same hash output value for the same input.

Algorithms Used for Generating Message Digests   MD5 and SHA-2 are the popular algorithms used for generating message digests.

> MD5: MD5 generates a 128-bit message digest in a four-step process. In the past few years, MD5 has been shown to be vulnerable to collisions and the (secure hash algorithm) SHA-2 algorithm is being preferred over MD5.
> SHA-2: SHA-2 is a highly secure algorithm that has been adopted by U.S. federal agencies as an information processing standard for use in their applications. SHA-2 consists of a set of four hashing functions that generate digests of 256, 224, 512, and 384 bits, respectively. One of the concerns with SHA-2 has been the limited operating system support for this algorithm.

When Should Message Digest Techniques Be Used?   This technique is more widely used in SSL and transmission of messages and rarely used for production dynamic masking scenarios (used only when the overwhelming concern is to ensure that the source data have not been altered).

Partial Sensitivity and Partial Masking

Not all characters in a sensitive field need to be anonymized. For example, the first 12 digits of a credit card number may be considered sensitive, whereas the last 4 digits may not be considered so. In such cases, it is not necessary to anonymize all the data and only the sensitive portion needs to be anonymized. In such cases, partial masking is used. Other than shuffling and nulling out techniques, all other basic anonymization techniques can be leveraged for partial masking. Table 16.16 explains the practical usage of partial masking.

Masking Based on External Dependancy

There are cases when data cannot be considered to be sensitive independently. The sensitivity of the data depends on one or more fields in the same table, another table, or another data store. Such cases merit

Table 16.16   Example of Partial Masking

Unmasked credit card number	1234567890123456
Partially masked credit card number	************3456

the usage of this type of masking, where data would be masked based on a condition being met. Here are some of examples:

(a) In a retail store database, mask the value of the Price column in the Commodity table to a standard value of 200 if the Supplier Shipment Date column in the same table is less than 30 days from the current date. This helps in keeping the prices of commodities during the last month confidential.

(b) In the employee database, set the award column to null wherever the corresponding National Awardee column has a value Y.

Auxiliary Anonymization Techniques

These are techniques where one or more basic anonymization technique is used for generating the anonymized value or the anonymization is wholly a custom implementation. Format-specific masking techniques like SSN (or National ID), string format, numeric format, phone number, and e-mail ID are all examples of auxiliary anonymization techniques. These techniques enable the preservation of the data format even after anonymization and leverage one or more basic anonymization techniques like substitution or cryptographic techniques. For example when a telephone number or National Identification Number is masked, the masked value would also need to have a separator character at the same position (as the unmasked value) as shown in Table 16.17.

Social Security Number (SSN) Masking Technique   The SSN, which is a unique national identification issued for both citizens and noncitizens in the United States, has an 11-character format (9 Numbers + 2 separator characters) that can be divided into three segments as shown in Table 16.18.

This technique generates an anonymized SSN value, which would still have the same format (as the input data), will be realistic, and still be an unused SSN.

Table 16.17 Example of
Format-Specific Masking

UNMASKED VALUE	MASKED VALUE
510-555-4432	201-678-3865

Table 16.18 SSN Format

AREA CODE		GROUP NUMBER		SERIAL NUMBER WITHIN THE GROUP
999	-	99	-	1565

Table 16.19 String Format-Masking Technique

	VALUE
Input (unmasked) value	AbcNY123
Target format specified for the technique (* indicates the characters to contain masked values)	***NY***
Output masked value using the string format-masking technique	a@bNY104

String Format-Masking Technique Many times there is a need to generate a masked string value as per a given format. The string format-masking technique is used in such scenarios. For example, if the need is to generate a string containing NY with three preceding and proceeding letters randomly, this technique is used as shown in Table 16.19. This technique identifies the characters to be masked in the string and generates a random character to replace the original character. NY will be left as it is.

Numeric Format-Masking Technique Many times there is a need to generate a masked numeric value as per a given format. The numeric format-masking technique is used in such scenarios. For example, if the need is to generate a string (say customer ID) containing NY with six proceeding numbers randomly, this technique is used as shown in Table 16.20. This technique identifies the numbers to be masked in the string and generates a random number to replace the original number. NY will be left as is.

Format-Specific Credit Card Masking Technique This technique is useful for generating realistic anonymized credit card numbers. This technique typically masks a portion of the credit card number but still generates a realistic credit card number.

Table 16.20 Numeric Format-Masking Technique

	VALUE
Input (unmasked) value	NY899045
Target format specified for the technique (* indicates the characters to contain masked values)	NY******
Output masked value using the numeric format-masking technique	NY044532

Table 16.21 Format-Specific Phone Number Masking Technique

DIGIT #	1	2	3	4	5	6	7	8	9	10	11	12
Unmasked input card number				-				-				
Algorithm for masking	Area code generally left unmasked			-		These digits are anonymized						

Phone Number Masking Technique This technique is useful for generating realistic anonymized phone numbers. Other than the first three digits of the phone number, the rest of the digits are masked while preserving the format of the phone number. As shown in Table 16.21, in a U.S.-specific phone number, the fourth and the eighth characters use "-" as the separator characters.

E-mail ID Masking Technique Using this technique for masking data will result in the format of the e-mail ID being preserved with the e-mail log-in, domain name, and suffix being separately masked and then concatenated. In Table 16.22, a random alphanumeric substitute with a variable length (say 3 to 15 characters) for e-mail log-in, domain name (say 3–10 characters), and suffix (say 2 to 8 characters) is generated separately and concatenated to form the anonymized value. This helps in the e-mail ID being realistic, but anonymized.

When Should Format-Specific Anonymization Techniques Be Used? These techniques are generally used when the generated anonymized values need to be realistic and the data need to be preserved. For example, if the need is to generate a realistic but anonymized social security

Table 16.22   Format-Specific E-Mail-ID Masking Technique

	E-MAIL LOG-IN	SEPARATOR CHARACTER	DOMAIN NAME	SEPARATOR CHARACTER	SUFFIX
Unmasked value	ram.singh	@	coffeebar	.	com
Masked value	john.devon	@	Syro	.	com

number, the social security number format-specific masking technique can be used to generate valid social security numbers.

Alternate Classification of Data Anonymization Techniques

Instead of classifying data anonymization techniques into basic techniques and auxiliary techniques, there are other schools of thought where the data anonymization techniques are broadly classified into substitution and translation techniques.

Substitution Techniques   Using substitution techniques, the data anonymization techniques generate anonymized data that are irreversible without keys and the generated anonymized data maintain relational data integrity. Instances of substitution techniques are: replacing all values of a sensitive column with a standard character or standard value, nulling out, or blanking out/removing out the sensitive value.

Translation Techniques   Here the generated anonymized value is reversible and will not maintain data integrity. Instances of translational techniques include:

XOR Encryption: This technique involves the application of bitwise XOR operator along with a binary key on the binary values of the input (de-anonymized) data to generate the anonymized value.

Alphanumeric Translation: Here the value is anonymized based on a one-to-one or positional mapping between different characters. For example, if ABCDE has a one-to-one mapping key FGHIJ, then an input value ABB would be anonymized to FGG using this technique.

The other translation techniques include numeric and date translations.

Leveraging Data Anonymization Techniques

Prerequisites   When applied on a database, anonymization techniques must ensure that the:

1. Anonymization does not alter the physical structure of the database.
2. Referential integrity of the data must be preserved (within a data store or across data stores).
3. Indexes, primary keys, and triggers are all intact after anonymization.

What Are the Techniques That Must Be Supported by Any Data Anonymization Tool?   In addition to supporting techniques for generating realistic masked data, the anonymization tool must also support techniques for generating gibberish-masked data (nonrealistic data), techniques (such as lookup techniques) for generating masked data of different lengths when compared to the original data, as well as cryptographic techniques (such as encryption and decryption) that allow the original value of data to be retrieved.

Measuring the Effectiveness of Anonymization Techniques   The effectiveness of the anonymization technique is based on the ease of "retrievability" of the original value from the anonymized value or "reversibility" of the anonymized data. The higher the chances of reversibility (of the anonymized data or the retrieval of the original data from anonymized data), the lower is the effectiveness of the anonymization technique. Thus substitution techniques always are more effective than translation techniques.

Key Considerations When Choosing a Data Anonymization Technique   Before choosing an anonymization technique, the objective of the anonymization must be clear. Choosing a technique can involve a trade-off between one or more of the following choices:

- Should the anonymized data be realistic?
- Should the anonymized data be repeatable independent of time or location?
- Should the length of the masked data be the same as the original data?

- Should the format of the anonymized field be preserved?
- Should relational integrity be preserved within the same data stores?
- Should relational integrity be preserved across multiple data stores?
- Should functional dependencies on specific values be maintained after anonymization?
- Should the anonymized data be reversible or should they be irreversible?
- Should a stronger anonymization technique be used?
- Is the field to be anonymized conditionally sensitive?
- Is the field to be anonymized partially sensitive?

Table 16.23 provides a ready-reckoner of the attributes of anonymization techniques and helps make a decision on which technique to choose.

Case Study

Let's take an example of an application that receives payment details from an upstream application through an input file, stores the data in the application database AppDB in a table, AppTable, and sends a notification to a downstream system through an Output File.

Input File Structure

The input file is of fixed format with characters 10 to 25 specifying the credit card number of the customer (who made the payment), characters 1 to 9 indicate the customer ID. The rest of the characters from 25 onward specify other fields that indicate nonsensitive fields like payment date, payment purpose, merchant ID, transaction ID, and payment amount.

AppTable Structure

The AppTable contains the customer ID, customer first name, customer last name, customer credit card number, transaction ID, and transaction amount columns.

Table 16.23 Anonymization Technique Ready-Reckoner

ANONYMIZATION TECHNIQUE	REALISTIC ANONYMIZED DATA	LENGTH OF THE MASKED DATA = LENGTH OF UNMASKED DATA	FORMAT OF THE MASKED DATA MUST BE PRESERVED	REPEATABLE ANONYMIZED DATA	IRREVERSIBILITY OF ANONYMIZED DATA	CRYPTOGRAPHICALLY STRONG	COMMENTS
Shuffling	X						Easy to guess the original unmasked data when used on small data sets
Group shuffling	X						Easy to guess the original unmasked data when used on small data sets
Substitution		X		X	X		Repeatable only if "deterministic or nonrandom algorithms are used"
Lookup substitution	X			X	X		Repeatable only if "deterministic or nonrandom algorithms are used"
Nulling out					X		

Technique						Repeatable anonymized data are generated if same key is used
Character masking		X			X	
Replacement with specific characters (string/literal)		X			X	
Removal of data (replacement with blank values)					X	
Encryption, decryption		X		X		X
Hashing		X		X		X
Date variance	X	X	X			
Number variance	X	X	X			
Random date variance	X	X	X		X	
Random number variance	X	X	X		X	
Format specific masking techniques (SSN, phone, e-mail, credit card)	X	X	X			

Table 16.24   Fields To Be Anonymized

DATA STORE	SENSITIVE FIELDS
Input file	Credit card number
Database (AppTable table in AppDB database)	Customer first name, customer last name, customer credit card number

Output File Structure

The output file is also of fixed format structure, with characters 1 to 9 being the Customer ID and characters 10 to 25 indicating the credit card number. The rest of the fields are insignificant for data anonymization.

The application analysis shows that the credit card number and customer IDs present in the input file, AppTable, and output file are all related. Customer ID is not considered sensitive in this example. The application sensitivity analysis determines that the sensitive fields that would need to be anonymized are shown in Table 16.24.

The objective of anonymization is to provide data for a testing environment where the input file would be manually retrieved from the production file archive before testing the application, and the database would be refreshed weekly from the production environment. The scope of the testing is limited to ensure that the output file is generated with the relevant data and that there is no need to further feed this file into the downstream application. Hence there is no requirement to unmask the credit card number in the output file.

Given the above context, these are the appropriate techniques that can be used for anonymizing the data in the input file as well as the AppTable. The user acceptance testers have demanded that if they need to test with anonymized data, the anonymized names of the customer need to be realistic.

Solution

Given that the customer names need to be realistic, the customer first name and customer last name can be anonymized by using either the shuffling (word) or lookup substitution techniques.

Given that the credit card number in the input file is related to the customer credit card number in the AppTable, the same deterministic masking technique will need to be used when anonymizing these fields in both the data stores in order to ensure that relational integrity is preserved across both the data stores.

Had there been a need to ensure that the credit card number field in the output field is unmasked before being passed to a downstream application, we would have used encryption as the technique with the same key for the credit card number field in the input file as well as the customer credit card number field in the AppTable. For unmasking the credit card number in the output file, we would also need to decrypt the credit card number field with the same key that was used for encrypting the credit card number values in the input file and the AppTable.

Thus it is clear that the choice of the anonymization technique depends on the context of the usage of the data, and any enterprise guideline for an anonymization technique application must accommodate this.

Conclusion

Anonymization techniques transform data from their original form to anonymized form. The basic anonymization techniques include substitution, number variance, date variance, nulling out, character masking, shuffling, and cryptographic techniques such as encryption, hashing, and the like. Most of the above techniques have further variations.

Other than shuffling and nulling out, all other techniques support partial masking of data, and other than shuffling, all other techniques support conditional masking of data. Applying encryption (cryptographic technique) and substitution can result in a repeatable or deterministic anonymized value or a random value.

One or more of the above basic anonymization techniques can be combined to form auxiliary anonymization techniques. Auxiliary anonymization techniques involve preceding or proceeding one or more basic anonymization techniques with activities such as formatting or evaluating conditions and rules. Auxiliary anonymization techniques can also be wholly custom-built techniques.

Data Anonymization Mandatory and Optional Principles

Mandatory Principles   Any anonymization technique must ensure that the data type of the resultant anonymized value is preserved. When applied on a database, anonymization must ensure that:

- The referential integrity of the original data set is preserved.
- The physical structure of the database is not altered.
- Indexes, primary keys, and triggers are all intact after anonymization.

Optional Principles   Some of the optional principles the anonymization techniques can follow include:

- Anonymized data need to be realistic (when there is no need for encryption).
- The length of anonymized data must match the length of the input (de-anonymized) data.
- The format of the anonymized data must match that of the input (de-anonymized) data.
- Anonymized data must be irretrievable.

Selection of Anonymization Techniques   Selecting the right anonymization technique to apply on unmasked data is based on answers to the following questions:

- What is the target environment for anonymization? Is it functional testing, integration testing, or for production environments or any other environments?
- Should the data be irretrievable or retrievable?
- Should the data be deterministic or random?
- Should referential integrity be preserved within and across the data store?
- Should the sensitive data be partially or conditionally masked?
- Should the data be realistic?
- Should the format of the data be preserved?

Reference

1. http://cis.poly.edu/~ross/networksecurity/Cryptography.ppt.

17

DATA ANONYMIZATION IMPLEMENTATION

Points to Ponder

- What are the prerequisites to be fulfilled before beginning data anonymization implementation?
- What are the activities involved in a data anonymization implementation for an application?
- What are the challenges and best practices of data anonymization implementation?

Data anonymization implementation projects are successful when they are aligned with enterprise privacy initiatives. Data anonymization needs to be an ongoing exercise throughout the life cycle of the application (even for minor enhancements of the application).

Ideally, the implementation of a data anonymization solution for any application must begin after the following prerequisites have been met:

- The enterprise is clear on the regulatory laws with which they need to comply.
- The data categories that need to be considered as sensitive and need not be considered sensitive have been determined and vetted by the legal team and security and risk teams of the enterprise.
- Data privacy governance and anonymization steering committee is in place and the committee includes unit-level representatives.
- Data security and privacy policies are in place.
- Data privacy and security incidence response management team and policies are in place.

For which application should anonymization first be started? (Courtesy of Jophy Joy)

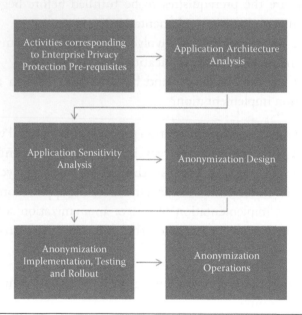

Figure 17.1 Phasewise data anonymization implementation approach for any application.

Before any big-bang anonymization implementation across the enterprise, most organizations implement a pilot data anonymization project for a representative application with the chosen anonymization tool to understand the challenges. Figure 17.1 provides a phasewise approach toward implementing data anonymization on any application.

As explained in Figure 17.1, a phasewise approach to data anonymization implementation involves the:

- *Application Architecture Analysis Phase* where the data sources, data stores, and data sinks of the application are identified.

- *Sensitivity Analysis Phase* where the sensitive elements of the application are identified and prioritized.
- *Anonymization Design Phase* where the techniques and solution pattern for treatment of sensitive fields are chosen.
- *Anonymization Implementation, Testing, and Rollout Phase* where
  - Masking jobs or scripts with the anonymization techniques are configured and executed.
  - Application is tested with anonymized data.
  - Anonymization process is integrated into the data flow process from production to nonproduction environments.
- *Operations phase* where anonymization is accommodated into the application enhancements and maintenance processes.

Prerequisites before Starting Anonymization Implementation Activities

Before beginning anonymization implementation activities of any application, the following prerequisites need to be met.

Sensitivity Definition Readiness—What Is Considered Sensitive Data by the Organization?

Sensitivity definition readiness in turn depends on legal readiness of the organization in terms of understanding the law's application to the enterprise as well as identification of the sensitive data domains handled by the enterprise.

Legal Readiness   Knowing the answers to the following questions indicates the legal readiness of the enterprise to embark on a data anonymization implementation.

- Is PCI-DSS relevant to the enterprise?
- Is European Data Privacy Protect Act relevant to the enterprise?
- Is HIPAA relevant to the enterprise?
- Which are the other data privacy laws relevant to the organization?

Sensitive Domain Data Prerequisites   Based on the understanding of the privacy regulations relevant to the enterprise, a list of domain fields that are considered to be sensitive is drawn up.

Sensitive Data Discovery—Where Do Sensitive Data Exist?

Sensitive data are received, transmitted, and stored across heterogeneous data stores by multiple applications across different environments. The sheer heterogeneity of the data sources makes the manual effort error prone. An automated approach leveraging a mix of network, port scanning tools, and data discovery tools can help discover the sources of sensitive data in a more efficient manner.

When, based on the enterprise's legal compliance requirements, guidelines around the data that must be considered sensitive exist and we know which are the applications receiving, storing, and transmitting sensitive data, the way is clear for data anonymization implementation of prioritized applications starting with one or more pilot applications with representative characteristics.

Sensitive Domain List   Figure 17.2 shows a sample list of domain fields that are generally considered sensitive by enterprises that need to comply with data privacy regulations.

Many financial and insurance industries receive or transmit payment files (like SWIFT) that contain sensitive information. A sample of the sensitive information typically found in these files is provided in Figure 17.3.

The sensitive domain lists in the figure must be treated more as a sample and not as an exhaustive list. Specific implementations may have additional sensitive fields. In the list of sensitive PII, some of these domain fields are partially sensitive and some of them are always sensitive. For example, employee name and contact details may also be found in the company's telephone directory and may not be considered sensitive by themselves. However, when they are used as part of a compensation system, they are sensitive.

Application Architecture Analysis

The application architecture analysis phase helps in scoping the data stores for which sensitivity analysis needs to be performed, arriving at the anonymization solution as well as defining how it will integrate with the application and its eco-system.

Sensitive Personal Information	Sensitive Financial Information	Sensitive Health Information	Sensitive Employee Information in HR Systems
• Name (Full Name, Short Name, First Name, Middle Name Last Name) • Address fields smaller than a state • Telephone/Fax Number (Home/ Work/Cell or Mobile number) • City, Area, County • Zip Code/Postal Index Number code (PINCode) • National Identification Number/ Social Security Number, National Insurance Number, Tax Identification Number • Contact Details • Dates related to personal identity (like Date of Birth, Date of Joining or Date of Admission, Date of Termination, Date of Death) • Birth Location Information • E-mail address/Social Networking ID • IP Address, Host Address, URL • Driver's License details • Certificate Number • Vehicle identifiers and serial numbers, including license plate numbers • Device Address/Identification Number • Any other Personal Identification Numbers like Passport Number, etc.	• Account Name • Account/Customer Block Reason • Credit History • Any Comments, Reason or Reference fields • Counterparty Details like Counterparty Name, Address, City, Zip Code/PIN Code, Phone, Fax, e-mail address, Social Networking ID, URL • Credit Card/Debit Card Information (CVV, Permanent Account Number, Card Number, Card Validity Dates)	• Medical record numbers • Health plan beneficiary numbers • Discharge Date/ Admission Date • Illness Details • Disability Information	• Disability • History/Work Experience • Date of Birth, Date of Joining, Date of Termination, Date of Death • Residential Address • Performance Evaluation History and details • Personal ID (SSN/Tax ID/Driving License details/ Certificate details) • Employment History and Prior Work History • Names and Contact Details (Phone, Fax, Social Networking IDs) • Nationality, Race, Religious preferences, sexual orientation, marital status, country of birth, ethnicity • Educational Details • Termination History, Details like reasons • Health Information and Medical History • Family Information, Dependent Information • Family Health Information/Dependent Health Information and Disability • Performance Details, Disciplinary Information, Grievances • Compensation details and incentives • Bank Account Information, Credit History, Background Verification Information • Absence details/reasons, Membership of any organizations • Habits like Smoking, Drinking • Personal IDs like Passport, Work Permit, Visa details

Figure 17.2 Sample sensitive personal information, health information, financial information, and sensitive employee information in HR systems.[7]

Sample Sensitive Information found in Payment files

{
- Order placing Customer or Institution
- Sender Information
- Beneficiary Information
- Bank Information
- Originator Information
- Sender's or Beneficiary's Financial Institution Information
- Sender-Beneficiary Communication Information
- Intermediary Information
- Intermediary Account number
}

Figure 17.3   Sample sensitive information typically found in payment files.

Scoping the data stores for sensitivity analysis would involve identifying the data sources, sinks, and stores of the application.

Arriving at the anonymization solution involves understanding how the data flows across the application as well as the application's technology stack.

In order to integrate the anonymization solution with the application and its eco-system, the integration architecture of the application needs to be understood. This involves identifying the upstream and downstream applications, how the current application receives data from upstream applications and transmits them to downstream applications, as well as the format and protocol for exchanging data with these applications.

Application Sensitivity Analysis

The objective of this exercise is to identify the sensitive fields handled (received, stored, and transmitted) by the application based on the enterprise sensitivity guidelines and sensitive domain fields; identify their format and data type; arrive at the sensitive data map for the application; and prioritize the sensitive fields for treatment as per their determined sensitivity level. This exercise provides the basis for identifying the anonymization technique for treatment of the sensitive field.

Sensitivity analysis needs to go beyond just identifying the sensitive fields of the application in order to provide a holistic treatment to sensitive fields in the application. The sensitivity analysis must also identify the fields related to sensitive data explicitly or implicitly.

SENSITIVE DATA MAP

A sensitive data map for an application is essentially a mapping between the sensitive data received by the application, the sensitive data stored by the application, and the sensitive data transmitted by the application to the downstream applications.

HOW DO SENSITIVE DOMAIN FIELDS TRANSLATE TO APPLICATION SENSITIVITY?

Domain fields serve as a template for identifying sensitive fields in the enterprise. Sensitive domain fields may be, say, name, national identification numbers, phone numbers, IP addresses, and the like, or reasons for absence of employee.

These domain fields translate to data store fields. For example, the domain "name" may translate into FIRST_NAME, LAST_NAME, CUST_NAME columns in the application database and these would turn out to be sensitive fields of the application.

Relationships between fields can be explicit (through referential integrity keys) or implicit (here the data are related more by external or hardcoded application business rules). While the explicitly defined referential integrity in databases is easy to detect, the same is not true for identification of the implicit relationship of the sensitive fields. Relationships can be within the data store or across data stores (say, between an input file received from an upstream application and the application database where these data are stored).

What Is the Sensitivity Level and How Do
We Prioritize Sensitive Fields for Treatment?

The sensitivity level can be classified as high, medium, or low. The higher the sensitivity level is, the higher the negative impact of any misuse of this data. Thus the higher the sensitivity level is, the stronger the techniques needed to anonymize the data.

The sensitivity level can be determined from the following list of parameters:[5]

Access and location of data: The more often the data are accessed (in their original form), the more vulnerable they are for misuse. The more the data are accessed from portable devices, the higher is the risk of misuse.

Identifiability of data: By identifiability, we answer the question: "If somebody gets hold of these data in their original form, how closely can the individual be identified?" For example, *SSN* or *Date of Birth* can directly identify a person whereas *Gender* or *City* may not identify the person so closely, given that the number of people associated with this *Gender* or *City* may be much larger.

Quantity of data exposed in case of potential misuse of the PII: Here we try to answer the question: "If somebody gets hold of these data in their original format, how many such records exist; that is, how many records are left open to misuse?" For example, if we have two million records with credit card numbers in original form (deanonymized form) we are running the risk of high penalties, multiple lawsuits, and a potential loss of two million customers in case we don't anonymize this field and there is any misuse of data.

Case Study

This case study provides an overview of how the sensitivity level for different fields is arrived at based on their context. Table 17.1 suggests a way to arrive at the sensitivity level of any sensitive field.

One of the approaches to arriving at the sensitive data vulnerability score is to simply sum up the vulnerability score for each of the sensitive fields as per context. Another popular approach is to allow the user to specify the weights for each of the contextual parameters and come up with the scores for the sensitive field to arrive at the sensitivity level.

The sensitivity level of the field can be arrived at based on Table 17.2.

Table 17.1   Sensitive Data Vulnerability Scoring Criteria

CONTEXTUAL PARAMETER	VULNERABILITY SCORING CRITERIA	VULNERABILITY SCORE
(Frequency) of access to data	Data are accessed at least once a month	1
	Data are accessed at least once a week	2
	Data are accessed at least once a day	3
Access location	Data are accessible by internal users from desktop computers within office premises	1
	Data are accessible by internal users over VPN/extranet through laptops/mobile enabled devices	2
	Data are accessible by external users over the Internet	3
Identifiability of data with the subject (person)	Person cannot be directly identified and belongs to a category with a large sample	1
	Person can be identified when combined with another field	2
	Person is directly identifiable	3
Quantity of data exposed in case of potential misuse	<25% of stakeholders (customers/employees) potentially exposed	1
	>25% and < = 50% of stakeholders (customers/employees) potentially exposed	2
	>50% of the stakeholders (customers/employees) potentially exposed	3

Table 17.2   Sensitive Level Ready Reckoner

SENSITIVE DATA VULNERABILITY SCORE	SENSITIVITY LEVEL
< = 4	Low
Between 4 and 8	Medium
Between 8 and 12	High

The sensitive level ready reckoner would not hold well if a weighted average approach were to be taken.

Let's determine the sensitivity of the following fields in an application based on an example. Table 17.3 shows the sensitive fields identified as part of a different table in the application database and their context of use. Based on the sensitive data vulnerability scoring criteria table, the scores for these sensitive fields would be as shown in Table 17.4. Based on the sensitivity level ready reckoner table, the sensitivity level for each of the sensitive fields in this example would be as shown in Table 17.5.

Table 17.3 Contextual Parameters for Sensitive Data for a Sample Application

SENSITIVE COLUMN	TABLE	DATA ACCESS	ACCESS LOCATION	IDENTIFIABILITY	QUANTITY
SSN	Customer	Daily	Accessed by internal user on desktop within intranet	Direct	>50% of customer data is stored in this application data store
Marital Status	Customer	Yearly	Accessed by internal user on desktop within intranet	Indirect	
Credit Card Number	Card	Weekly	Accessed by internal user on desktop within intranet	Direct	
First Name	Customer	Daily	Accessed by internal user on desktop within intranet	Needs to be associated with Last Name for identifying person	
First Name	Employee Admin	Monthly	Accessed by internal user on mobile device	Needs to be associated with Last Name for identifying person	10% of employee names

Table 17.4   Sensitive Data Vulnerability Score for the Given Example

SENSITIVE COLUMN	TABLE	DATA ACCESS	ACCESS LOCATION	IDENTIFIABILITY	QUANTITY	TOTAL SCORE
SSN	Customer	3	1	3	3	10
Marital Status	Customer	1	1	1	3	6
Credit Card Number	Card	2	1	3	3	9
First Name	Customer	3	1	2	3	9
First Name	Employee Admin	1	2	2	1	6

Table 17.5   Sensitivity Level for the Example

SENSITIVE COLUMN	TABLE	SENSITIVITY LEVEL
SSN	Customer	High
Marital Status	Customer	Medium
Credit Card Number	Card	High
First Name	Customer	High
First Name	Employee Admin	Medium

Thus SSN, Credit Card Number, and First Name columns in the Customer table need to be anonymized using an anonymization technique of higher strength than Marital Status and First Name columns of the Employee table.

In addition to the quantitative contextual parameters for determining sensitivity level of the field, the usage context also plays an important part in determining the sensitivity level, although this cannot be a quantitative metric.

From the above example it is clear that:

- The sensitivity level of any sensitive field depends on the context of use.
- The same sensitive field can have a different sensitivity level for a different context.

Usage context can be defined as the reason behind why the sensitive data are being handled by the application. Usage context examples include research, statistical analysis, tax administration, benefits eligibility, and administration or law enforcement.

Thus if the same set of sensitive fields is used for different use cases such as:

1. For communication to customers/prospects who have volunteered for subscription to the mailing list
2. For identifying people who work as intelligence personnel of the nation

then the list identifying people who work as intelligence personnel would have a higher sensitivity level when compared to the list identifying people who have subscribed for mailing lists.

> # WHAT IS THE DIFFERENCE BETWEEN DATA CLASSIFICATION LEVEL AND SENSITIVITY LEVEL? AREN'T THEY THE SAME?
>
> The data classification level helps only in determining if the data are sensitive or not.
>
> The sensitivity level is determined after it is established that the data are sensitive. This helps in determining whether stronger techniques are needed for anonymization or weaker techniques would be sufficient.

The key deliverable of a sensitivity analysis phase would be the sensitivity analysis report. The sensitivity analysis report specifies the list of sensitive data stores, data sinks and sources for the application, the sensitive fields in each of these sensitive repositories, their metadata-like data type, length, format, their related fields in the same or different repository, and the sensitivity level.

Anonymization Design Phase

In this phase we arrive at the specific techniques to be used for anonymization of each sensitive field and the anonymization pattern to be used.

Choosing an Anomymization Technique for
Anonymization of Each Sensitive Field

Arriving at the specific technique to be used for anonymization begins with the implementation of the enterprise guidelines on techniques to be chosen for anonymizing sensitive domain fields. These guidelines are further fine-tuned as per the sensitivity analysis report and sensitive data flow map.

In addition to adhering to the broad guidelines on techniques to be used for anonymizing data, the specific technique to be used for anonymization depends on the answers to the following questions:

- What is the sensitivity level of the data?
- Which are the conditionally sensitive fields and partially sensitive fields?
- Should the anonymization technique result in irretrievable data?
- Should the values generated be random or should they be deterministic?
- Is the sensitive data field independent? Or is there any relational integrity with other tables? Is the referential integrity explicitly defined or is it through implicit application rules?

Choosing a Pattern for Anonymization

Arriving at the pattern to be selected for the anonymization solution depends on the answers to the following questions:

- What is the purpose of anonymization? Is this to provide anonymized data for nonproduction environments such as testing and development or is this to provide anonymized data to production environments?
- If the purpose of anonymization is for providing anonymized data for testing, what are the different types of testing for which these data are needed?
- What is the existing process for moving data from production to nonproduction environments?
- How should the anonymization process be integrated with the existing data flow?

As a deliverable of this phase, we should have the anonymization solution ready for implementation.

Table 17.6   Choosing an Anonymization Solution Based on Sensitive Data Flow

APPLICATION RECEIVES SENSITIVE DATA	APPLICATION STORES SENSITIVE DATA	APPLICATION TRANSMITS SENSITIVE DATA	ENVIRONMENTAL PATTERN CHOSEN
	X		Standalone anonymization environment
X	X	X	Automated integration environment or scaled-down integration test environment
X			Scaled-down integration test environment

SENSITIVE DATA FLOW MAP

The sensitive data flow map that portrays how sensitive data are received, stored, and transmitted helps arrive at the first-level design of the anonymization solution. The following question is answered by discovering the sensitive data flow map:

- What type of environment is needed for an integration test to be performed using Anonymized Data?

Table 17.6 helps in choosing the environmental anonymization patterns based on how the application handles sensitive data.

Thus Table 17.6 indicates that:

- When an application only stores sensitive data, a standalone anonymization environment is sufficient.
- When an application only receives sensitive data, a scaled-down integration test environment (for anonymization) is needed.
- When an application receives, stores, and transmits sensitive data, an automated integrated test environment, or scaled-down integration test environment (for anonymization) is the right environment.

Anonymization Implementation, Testing, and Rollout Phase

This phase involves the following activities:

- Configuring the anonymization tool with a set of anonymization rules.
- Creation and execution of anonymization jobs.
- Advising the information technology (IT)/security group on the controls needed for the anonymization environment.
- Implementation of these controls in the anonymization environment.
- Sharing the evidence of anonymization with information security/risk management groups. Most organizations that have an enterprise information security and risk management function mandate that evidence of anonymization of data be presented to them before they provide a sign-off.
- Certification by application testers that the application behavior has not changed due to the usage of anonymized data.
- Creation of operations manual.
- Training those personnel who would be regularly anonymizing data for future application enhancements is also part of this phase.

TERMS USED IN ANONYMIZATION IMPLEMENTATION

Anonymization Rule: This is the mapping of the anonymization technique to be used for each sensitive field.

Anonymization Script: This is the set of anonymization rules to be used on specified data store elements.

Anonymization Configuration: This contains the connection string to connect to the sensitive data store and the details of which job has to execute which anonymization script.

Anonymization Job: The anonymization job executes the anonymization scripts as specified in the anonymization configuration. The anonymization configuration may also contain the schedule for the job to run

This phase is assumed to be complete after the testing team has certified that testing with anonymized data has not changed the behavior of the application.

Anonymization Controls

The following are the objectives for applying anonymization controls (when the use case of anonymization is to provide data to nonproduction environments):

- No data should leave the production environment without anonymization.
- Production data should be not be accessible to unauthorized users.
- Any keys used for anonymization must not be accessible from nonproduction environments or to unauthorized individuals.

OPERATIONS MANUAL

In addition to an established process for anonymization, the deliverable of this phase would include an operations manual. This operations manual details the step-by-step process for anonymization and security controls for the anonymization process, apart from guidelines on how to incorporate the anonymization process into the application enhancement and maintenance process.

The anonymization controls are:

- Anonymization tool must be accessible only within the firewall (i.e., before data leave the production environment).
- Anonymization process must be executed only within the firewall (i.e., before data leave the production environment).
- Key management controls:
  - The keys used for anonymization should not be accessible outside the firewall (i.e., outside the anonymization environment) and must be stored in an access-controlled secure environment.

- The keys used for anonymization should be available only to authorized users and must be periodically refreshed (say once every six months).

Anonymization Operations

The objectives of the anonymization operations phase are:

- Stabilize the anonymization processes.
- Ensure that any application enhancements or bug-fixes incorporate the anonymization processes as part of the life cycle.

Application fixes or enhancements that do not involve any data schema change or any new field being introduced for processing do not require any anonymization process changes.

For those fixes that involve data changes, the following process (Figure 17.4) needs to be incorporated into the application software development/maintenance/enhancement/bug-fix life cycle:

From Figure 17.4, it is clear that:

- When a new data element is added and is considered sensitive, the anonymization configuration/rule sets must include the new anonymization rule (specify the sensitive data element as well as the technique for anonymizing the data element). An impact analysis of the relationships of this data element also

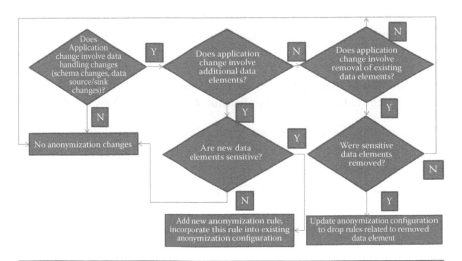

Figure 17.4 Impact of application changes on anonymization process.

needs to be considered and the anonymization configuration must be appropriately updated.

- When a new data element is added and is not considered sensitive, there is no change to the anonymization process or configuration.
- When an existing data element is removed and this data element is sensitive, the anonymization configuration/rule sets must be updated to remove any anonymization rule that involves this data element. An impact analysis of the relationships of this data element also needs to be considered and the anonymization configuration must be appropriately updated.
- When an existing data element is removed and this data element is not considered sensitive, there is no change to the anonymization process or configuration.

INCREMENTAL MASKING

In most use cases, only static data require anonymization and transactional data rarely require anonymization. Thus, for any application that undergoes frequent bug-fixes/patch-fixes or slightly less frequent enhancements, it is necessary that the anonymization tool support incremental masking. Always needing a full dump of anonymized data from production is not feasible and thus having the ability to provide an incremental dump of masked data from a specific date onwards (which is generally the last date of refresh from production) is a must for any anonymization tool.

Incorporation of Privacy Protection Procedures as Part of Software Development Life Cycle and Application Life Cycle for New Applications

With the need for data privacy protection having legal repercussions for the well-being of the organization, we need to incorporate privacy protection activities into the software development life cycle (SDLC) and application life cycle (ALC). Figure 17.5 depicts the interaction of SDLC and ALC.

From an SDLC perspective, the life cycle starts with requirements gathering and elaboration before it moves to the design, build, and testing phases. At the end of testing, the application moves to

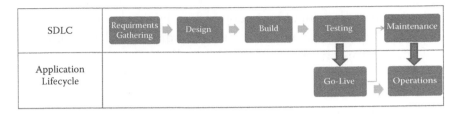

Figure 17.5   Interaction between SDLC and application life cycle.

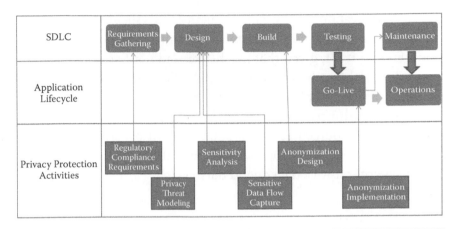

Figure 17.6   Incorporation of privacy protection activities into SDLC and application life cycle for new applications.

production (go-live). Any changes, fixes, or enhancements needed in production are provided as part of the maintenance phase activities.

From an ALC perspective, until the application goes live on production, it can be assumed to be more at a conceptual stage (not depicted in the figure). The life cycle can be considered to have begun when it is goes live in production. Once the application becomes stable, it gets into the operations phase (which can also be outsourced to third parties (BPO)).

Once the anonymization process is established in the organization, it is necessary to incorporate data privacy protection practices into the SDLC and ALC of new applications. Figure 17.6 depicts how this can be done. Thus as shown in the figure:

- The requirements gathering and elaboration phase must include specification of the regulatory compliance requirements for the application.
- During the design phase, just as with security threat modeling, it is also necessary to conduct a privacy threat modeling

exercise. This should be followed up by sensitivity analysis activities and the sensitive data flow must also be captured during this phase.

- At the end of the build phase, we can take up the anonymization design activities to identify the techniques and patterns as part of the anonymization solution.

The key objective is to have the anonymization implemented by the time the application goes live in production. This should help mitigate the risk of misuse of sensitive data at beginning stages of the application life cycle itself, given that patch-fixes and hot-fixes are more frequent during the early stages of the application life cycle as compared to later stages when it becomes relatively stable.

We should also consider the possibility of the application management being outsourced at a later stage to third parties and as far as possible, ensure that the application design also addresses any potential misuse of sensitive data due to outsourcing.

Impact on SDLC Team

Given that proactively addressing privacy protection practices as part of the SDLC and ALC of any application requires additional effort, it is recommended that an additional member who is well versed in using the anonymization tool as well as data privacy protection aspects becomes part of the application team. The person playing this role would need to spend a significant amount of time interfacing with legal representatives, unit security officers, and the information security and risk management team.

Challenges Faced as Part of Any Data Anonymization Implementation

Implementing an enterprisewide data anonymization program comes with its own challenges. Here is a recap of typical challenges.

General Challenges

- There are too many stakeholders and multiple regulations for data privacy. Who should be held accountable? Which regulation is relevant to the organization?

- The more multinational and multilocational the nature of the organization, the higher the risk of data loss for the organization, as well as the more the number of regulations with which the organization needs to be compliant. How should we deal with the task of adhering to global as well as local regulations?

Functional, Technical, and Process Challenges

- *Functional dependency challenges*: What should be done when the application behavior depends on a fixed value of a sensitive field? Should we go ahead with anonymizing this field

PRIVACY THREAT MODELING

A privacy threat modeling exercise is about identification of the areas from where the threat of misuse of sensitive data arises. This exercise helps in taking precautionary measures against any misuse of sensitive application data.

Privacy threat modeling involves identification of:

- How the application will be used
- Who are the end users of the application
- How frequently the end users would use this application
- Devices and networks on which the users would be using this application
- What data would be accessible and editable by the authorized end users
- What are the potential use cases of unauthorized access of the application data
- Which are the vulnerable points of misuse
- The sensitive data that would be received, stored, and transmitted by the application
- The sensitive data that would be accessible by authorized and unauthorized users

and ignore the behavioral change or should we not anonymize this field? In such scenarios, nonsubstitution and nontranslation techniques would have to be explored.

- *Inadequate time spent on application analysis and sensitivity analysis*: This results in an inappropriate choice of anonymization techniques and results in more testing cycles and more time being spent on testing with anonymized data, as well as a longer time for implementation go-live. An anonymization implementation where the application analysis and sensitivity analysis have been adequately done would need just one or two cycles of testing whereas on the other side of the spectrum, even four to five cycles of testing do not ensure that application behavior remains unchanged with anonymized data.

- *Handling data elements with ambiguous sensitivity levels*: As part of auditing requirements, most application databases have fields named *createdby* or *lastupdatedby* that contain user names or employee log-ins. These fields do not provide any direct identifiability; however, there is always a remote chance that an insider who is motivated to misuse confidential data can contact the employee who had created or updated the field and get some amount of sensitive information out through social engineering practices or other activities. Should these fields be nulled out or replaced with blanks? The other challenge is in handling free text fields. These fields generally contain comments from users that may or may not be sensitive. It would always be advisable to err on the side of caution and blank out or null out these fields.

- *Separating the application issues from issues arising out of the use of anonymized data*: This issue relates back to the functional dependency challenges. If the application depends on hardcoded values of sensitive fields, this issue is bound to arise. If the application dependencies on the hardcoded values of sensitive fields are not identified before testing the anonymization implementation, it would be very difficult to separate the issues genuinely arising from application changes as against issues due to the use of anonymized data.

- *Availability of separate environments for anonymization*: Given the budget constraints faced by IT departments, availability of a separate environment for testing anonymization implementation is a major bottleneck. Nonavailability of separate environments during anonymization implementation always results in interference with application hot-fix releases and results in delays in the completion of anonymization implementation. A better approach would be to budget for provisioning a separate environment for anonymization implementation as part of the planning phase itself.

People Challenges

- *Getting a sign-off from application testers certifying that using anonymized data has not affected the behavior of the application*: Testers are always busy and testing application releases and hot-fixes always takes priority over any other requirements. However planned the implementation is, there is always one or another hot-fix that takes away the testers assigned for testing the anonymization implementation. This keeps delaying the final sign-off from the testers.
- *Getting a buy-in from the testing team for testing the application with anonymized data going forward*: On any day, testers are more comfortable testing with original data from production than with anonymized data. When we mention "anonymized" data, the first thought that strikes the minds of the testers is that all the fields in the test data set are going to be encrypted and they would not be able to make out what they are testing. Even when testers are reluctantly made to test with anonymized data, any new issue that crops up is always blamed on the data being anonymized and not on the application fixes.

In many organizations, acceptance test users get a buy-in from senior management to test the application with actual production data. The reasons provided are that they are trustworthy people anyway who do not intend or have never misused sensitive data and use of anonymized data affects their productivity. This issue can be addressed only by early engagement of testers in the anonymization implementation.

Best Practices to Ensure Success of Anonymization Projects

In addition to having enterprisewide privacy protection governance models, reusable processes for anonymization, enterprisewise guidelines for privacy protection, sensitive data identification, and anonymization technique selection, the following practices improve the success ratio of anonymization projects.

Creation of an Enterprise-Sensitive Data Repository

An enterprise-sensitive data repository that captures the sensitive fields identified as part of application sensitivity analysis for each application improves productivity of anonymization implementation projects. Given that multiple applications share the same databases and many fields are repeated across application data stores, an enterprisewide sensitive data repository strengthens reuse. It is, however, necessary to have a management application over this repository to ensure that this repository is updated by authorized users after due approvals.

Engaging Multiple Stakeholders Early

If system and acceptance testers are engaged early in the application anonymization implementation exercise, it helps them overcome their reluctance to use anonymized data by keeping them better informed about anonymization and addressing their concerns about the use of anonymized data.

Incorporating Privacy Protection Practices into SDLC and Application Life Cycle

This helps in ensuring that any changes to the application involving sensitive data do not result in the introduction of any loophole for misuse of sensitive data.

Conclusion

Certain prerequisites such as legal readiness and identification of sensitive data domains handled by the organization must be met before beginning the data anonymization implementation for an application. A phased manner of anonymization implementation includes the application architecture analysis phase, sensitivity analysis phase, anonymization design, anonymization implementation, and testing followed by the anonymization operations phase.

The efforts taken to implement data anonymization will not be a success unless the application enhancement or maintenance process is also integrated with the data anonymization process. Implementing data anonymization for any application comes with its own set of functional, technical, process, and people challenges. Following best practices of anonymization will help overcome some of these challenges.

References

1. Camouflage (http://doc.wowgao.com/ef/presentations/PPCamouflage. ppt)
2. *Guardian* (http://www.guardian.co.uk/healthcare-network/2011/may/04/personal-data-breaches-london-nhs-trusts-data)
3. *Guardian* (http://www.guardian.co.uk/healthcare-network/2011/may/04/biggest-threat-nhs-data-security-staff)
4. Datalossdb (http://www.datalossdb.org)
5. NIST (*Guide to Protecting the Confidentiality of Personally Identifiable Information*)
6. *USA Today* (cybercrime forum) (http://www.usatoday.com/tech/news/computersecurity/infotheft/2006-10-11-cybercrime-hacker-forums_x.htm)
7. NIH (http://privacyruleandresearch.nih.gov/pdf/HIPAA_Booklet-4-14-2003.pdf)

Appendix A: Glossary

Abbreviations

ALC: Application life cycle
BPO: Business process outsourcing
CFO: Chief financial officer
CIO: Chief information officer
CPO: Chief privacy officer
EAL: Extract-anonymize-load, a pattern associated with static masking
e.g.: For example
ELA: Extract-load-anonymize, a pattern associated with static masking
etc.: Et cetera
IT: Information technology
JDBC: Java database connector
p.a.: Per annum
RDBMS: Relational database management system
SDLC: Software development life cycle
SIT: System integration test
UAT: User acceptance test
UI: User interface

Terms Used in Anonymization

Classified information: Information restricted to few authorized users.

Controlled environment: Application environment where sensitive data are available but restricted to necessary users.

Cryptography[1]

- **Asymmetric cipher:** Different keys used for encryption and decryption.
- **Brute Force Attack**[2]**:** The attacker tries different keys until the right key used to encrypt data is found. The higher the key length, the more difficult or time-consuming it is for the attacker to find the right key.
- **Cipher or cryptographic system:** A scheme for encryption and decryption.
- **Cipher text:** Encrypted message.
- **Cryptanalysis:** Science of studying attacks against cryptographic systems.
- **Cryptography:** Science of studying ciphers.
- **Cryptology:** Cryptography + cryptanalysis.
- **Deciphering or decryption:** Recovering plaintext from cipher text.
  - **Decryption algorithm:** Performs decryption and involves two inputs: cipher text and secret key.
- **Enciphering or encryption:** Process of converting plaintext into cipher text.
  - **Encryption algorithm:** Performs encryption and involves two inputs: a plaintext and a secret key.
- **Known plaintext attack**[1]**:** Attacker tries to decipher the key used for encrypting/decrypting data from the plaintext and cipher text pair.
- **Plaintext:** Original message to be encrypted.
- **Secret key:** Same key used for encryption and decryption. Also referred to as a symmetric key.
- **Symmetric cipher:** Same key used for encryption and decryption.
  - **Block cipher:** Encrypts a block of plaintext at a time (typically 64 or 128 bits).
  - **Stream cipher:** Encrypts data one bit or one byte at a time.

Data confidentiality: When only the sender and intended receiver can "understand" the transmitted message contents, data confidentiality is preserved. Typically the sender encrypts the message and the receiver decrypts it to preserve data confidentiality.

Data subsetting: Generating a logically related subset of data from original data. Data should be self-sufficient and complete for a particular use case.

Data tokenization: Process of generating tokenized values in place of actual personal data.

Decryption: Technique of getting back the original data from ciphertext using the key used for encryption.

Deterministic masking: Process of generating the same masked value as output at any point of time or location for the same input value.

Downstream system/application: The system or application to which the current system in scope must provide output data (as part of integration architecture).

Dynamic anonymization environment: In this environment, the integration test is enabled using anonymized data. Sensitive data in input files are masked before being processed by the current application. Thus a dynamic anonymization environment consists of one or more upstream applications feeding data to the current application which in turn may feed data to one or more downstream applications. The data anonymization process is seamlessly integrated with the end-to-end application data flow.

Dynamic masking: Anonymization of data in motion (Web service, Webpage data).

Encryption: Technique of converting data to an unreadable ciphertext using a key.

Gold copy: Master data subset which is a baseline for datasets for application development and testing.

Key Management: Management of the keys used for encryption.

Masked environment: Application environment containing production replica with sensitive information masked.

Mnemonics: Associations that can be related back to original data. For example, the mnemonic of a customer name would be customername_CustID.

Partial masking: Process of masking or anonymizing only a few characters in the data field.

PHI: Protected health information of an individual such as illness, duration of illness, and so on.

PII: Personally identifiable information such as SSN, DOB, credit card number, and so on. Information that can directly or indirectly enable identification of an individual.

Policies: Discuss what is to be done and are usually generic in nature.

Procedures: Discuss how this is to be done and are fairly specific.

Pseudonymization: Process by which original data are replaced with false data. However, this data value can be traced back to original data value. In anonymization, the original data value cannot be traced back.

Reverse masking: Process of unmasking or getting back the original value from masked value.

Sensitive information: Any information, which when revealed to unauthorized users, can potentially result in either loss of privacy of customers, employees, or partners and potential harm to them or loss of reputation, competitive advantage, or business for the organization can be termed sensitive information. PII, PHI, proprietary data, and internal financial and legal data of the organization can all be deemed sensitive although their sensitivity level or degree of sensitivity may vary.

Sensitivity analysis: Process of identifying sensitive data as per regulations across a data store or multiple data stores.

Static anonymization environment: In this environment anonymization is done for data-at-rest (data residing in databases).

Static masking: Anonymization of data at rest (data in database, files etc.).

Test data creation: Process for creating a logically related data set of false data for testing out the application.

Test data management: Comprises the processes, tools, and technology around test data creation, data masking, and data subsetting.

Uncontrolled environment: Application environment where sensitive information has been de-identified and can generally be a subset of production data.

Upstream system/application: The system or application providing input data to the current system in scope (as part of integration architecture).

Table A.1   Anonymization Technique Selection Decision Matrix

TYPE OF SENSITIVE FIELD	ANONYMIZATION TECHNIQUE CHOSEN	COMMENTS
Independent field (no relation with any other field)	Any technique (deterministic or nondeterministic) relevant for the datatype (to which the field belongs)	For example, a date field such as DOB may need an anonymization technique such as DateVariance Technique that can be used whereas the Firstname field can have a lookup technique for replacing the first name with a fictitious but realistic name.
Related field (referential integrity only across database)	Any deterministic anonymization technique relevant for the datatype (to which the field belongs)	For example, if the Firstname column in Customer Table and CustFname in Account table are related, any deterministic anonymization technique would result in the same value for the related fields.
Related field (referential integrity across the input data sources)	Any deterministic anonymization technique relevant for the datatype (to which the field belongs)	For example, if Firstname is present in Customer Table as well as part of the input feed file, any deterministic anonymization technique would result in the same value for the related fields.
Related field (referential integrity across input and output data stores)	Deterministic encryption technique has to be used. The key for encryption and decryption used must be the same	If the sensitive field has to be unmasked before being fed to the downstream application, then it would have to be decrypted using the same key (as that used in encryption).
Related field (referential integrity across output data sources)		The sensitive field will be left as is, if it can be passed through to the downstream system and the downstream system uses the same anonymization tool for masking. If the anonymization tool is different, then the sensitive field has to be unmasked before being fed to the downstream application, and it would have to be decrypted using the same key (as that used in encryption). The decrypted value is then fed on to the anonymization tool used for downstream application for anonymization.

Commonly Used Guidelines for Anonymizing Sensitive Domain Fields

Table A.1 summarizes the considerations behind selection of the anonymization technique for a sensitive field.

References

1. Classical Encryption, http://www.cse.ohio-state.edu/~lai/651/
2. Wikipedia, http://www.wikipedia.org

Index